T0165477

Empower Your Inner Manager

Empower Your Inner Manager

Essential Skills, Self-Assessment, and Effective Planning That Secure Successful Careers

Ian R. Mackintosh

iUniverse, Inc.
Bloomington

Empower Your Inner Manager
Essential Skills, Self-Assessment, and Effective
Planning That Secure Successful Careers

iUniverse books may be ordered through booksellers or by contacting:

iUniverse
1663 Liberty Drive
Bloomington, IN 47403
www.iuniverse.com
1-800-Authors (1-800-288-4677)

ISBN: 978-1-4759-2800-6 (sc)
ISBN: 978-1-4759-2802-0 (e)

Library of Congress Control Number: 2012909143

Printed in the United States of America

iUniverse rev. date: 05/30/2012

Contents

List of Tables

Preface

Why You Need to Read This Book

Many books on the market teach specific management training skills. This book is not intended to teach you how to gain or develop those skills. And be aware that some of those skills can be taught, some can be gained experientially, and some are simply innate. Regardless of the state of your skill set, this book *will* show you how to assess your skills and formulate an effective plan for your career development.

Now that you know what this book will and will not do, let's examine how it will fulfill its promised intentions. In a nutshell, it will show you how to target management positions, assess the skills you need in order to optimize your candidacy, target only the skills needed to improve, and develop a personalized plan to effect the necessary improvements. End result: getting the job you seek!

Similarly, you can also apply these principles to self-employment, entrepreneurship, and/or personal development, if you wish. This book will primarily focus on career development, but feel free to extend the principles presented to assist you in any area of personal development that resonates for you. Only you know what your

1

current goals and objectives are, and so you are the best person to perform your assessment and plan. Whatever your goals and objectives might be, above all, remember that good management always leads to lasting success, so assessing your management skills and designing your plan to best utilize them can only improve your effectiveness in both your career and your personal life.

Throughout, I will emphasize and reemphasize key points. Please indulge me in this, as my intention is not to be repetitive or redundant, but rather to ensure that you remain mindful of those principles that I have seen lead to success, time and time again. With that said, let me reemphasize the personalized plan. This book offers a unique process suited to your needs. Once you honestly complete the skills assessment, you can customize this book's advice to help you effectively attain your goals. Best of all, you can use the book multiple times throughout your career, whenever you feel the need to further develop your skills in order to seek a more attractive position. Indeed, even if you only use this book to expand your awareness of and insight into skills possessed by well-developed managers, you can benefit significantly. By choosing to invest in your development and awareness at any level, you improve your marketability and value.

How to Stand Out in Today's Ultracompetitive Job Market

Competition for management jobs continues to intensify with each passing year. If you are betting your financial welfare on your next management position and subsequent promotions, you will now need to be much better prepared to capture those increasingly scarce opportunities than you might previously have realized.

In a global economy, not only are professional jobs dispersed domestically and around the world, but, inevitably, so is the management of those positions. This does not bode well for us as managers seeking enhanced opportunities within our own communities. We already see job compression at the lowest levels, where increasingly competitive situations in many industries mean that even very competent graduates sometimes now struggle to find initial footings in their chosen fields. The swelling ranks of globally accessible well-qualified professionals mean that this compression feeds up through to the highest levels of the management chain. Those coveted top positions that were always difficult to secure have become both fewer and harder to capture.

In all likelihood, you are already aware of these dynamics. How, then, can you best prepare yourself for career opportunities? In the past, it might have been enough in an expanding industry to just show up and do your job well. You would be "patted on the back" for your achievements and could then expect reasonable promotions throughout your career as your company grew. This is really no longer the case. Industries are more mature now, which results in their often experiencing slowed growth and associated reduced expansion opportunities. And that means greater job competition. Compounding this, equally qualified coworkers abound. As a result, previously available management positions are lost because they are also often geographically dispersed in order to take advantage of other local markets and labor, as well as offshoring. You clearly cannot rely on such a random process for your own advancement in such a competitive environment. How, then, do you beat the system so that you can maximize your opportunities and excel in your field? The answer must be by maximizing the value you offer.

Avoiding Deselection

The good news is that the opportunity for success lies within your own hands. It is possible for you to develop and present yourself in such a

3

way that your selection for that next management opportunity can become more controllable, even inevitable. And certainly better than the often seemingly random selection "handed down from on high" for that choice position. The trick is to develop value that makes your appointment inevitable, and at the same time and most importantly, that eliminates or minimizes traits that could otherwise cause your "deselection." Where there are several qualified candidates for a position, the risk of deselection for weaknesses may be as great a risk as your enhanced skills are an opportunity.

The development of skills and minimization of weaknesses on your part naturally requires some effort. It is important that you train and develop yourself, rather than wait for the natural evolution of your current work to magically develop the skills and traits you need. In fact, your day-to-day job likely will not accomplish any of that. Indeed, studies have found that many people working in the same role for numerous years just become expert in that role, and yet never really develop beyond its associated and required set of skills and capabilities.[1] Even folks treading water in long-term management roles must consider self-development methods in order to ensure that they retain their competitive value as time rolls on!

Importantly, if you wish to advance, this means that you need to plan a path to acquire those skills and behaviors necessary to make your selection for that next management position inevitable. You must be perceived as already capable in that new role in order to make your selection more certain. One of the great surprises in most industries and businesses is that we generally don't prepare people for the next position; rather, we take a more remedial approach. When

---

1 Geoff Colvin, *Talent Is Overrated: What Really Separates World-Class Performers from Everybody Else,* paperback ed. (New York: Penguin, 2010), 2–4.

they are appointed to a position, we review their deficiencies and then begin to plan a program to "fix them" so that they will be more effective in that new role. Not a very productive system, especially if the fixes don't work out as planned! There are exceptions in some large corporations, where a little proactive training of individuals does occur; however, not everybody gets on those programs, nor do they all benefit from such opportunities. Therefore, it behooves us as individuals to take our futures into our own hands and define the productive training and development that we need. We must set a simple course of action to ensure that it is *we* who have the particular skills in place when we need them, so they are both visible and attractive when those great new job opportunities appear.

And again, remember, this book will show you how to assess your skills and formulate your plan based on honest analysis; it is not designed to teach you how to develop the skills you lack.

Honest Self-Assessment

In general, we cannot develop ourselves unless we are taken out of our comfort zone. Just as the drone worker or manager continues to do the same task day in day out with the inevitable risk of little personal development, so must we find a way to develop ourselves, to separate ourselves from the herd. It is only by taking ourselves out of our daily practices and seeking ways to develop ourselves that we will effect an improvement. Critically, we have to first understand how we need to develop and why. This means we must assess ourselves in the simplest manner and figure out in which key skills we excel, which we possess sufficiently, and which we may need to improve in order to bring them up to par.

No manager is perfect, which means that we all require some development. It is inevitable that we, as managers, seek to perfect our skills, especially if we wish to maximize our opportunities. No matter what level you have risen to as a manager, from first-line appointments through company CEOs, there will always be major areas in which you can improve. Occasionally, our very weaknesses in particular areas can actually be assets for a role, but in general it is better that we all are *aware* of our strengths and weaknesses, our mastery, adequacy, and any true deficiency. In this way, we can best position ourselves for career alternatives and make ourselves the "most desirable candidate" for new management positions and business/promotion opportunities. At the very least, our improved skills and increased awareness will certainly ensure our personal growth and valuable development for the long-term!

Key Points to Remember

Developing an understanding of your specific self-development needs is the purpose of this book. It will also provide you with a simple and effective listing, insight, awareness, and basic description of those foundational management skills needed. This will then enable you to quickly prioritize and determine where you must focus your own development, because you will be aware of your current mastery, adequacy, and deficiency in all key areas. With this plan in hand, you can then determine how to gain/develop the skills you lack while simultaneously making the most of the skills you do have, so that you don't lose or waste precious time.

Ian R. Mackintosh *has more than thirty years of management experience, which serves as the basis for the principles and recommendations that this book offers. Ian's mission in writing this book is to help managers of all levels effectively optimize their careers—and to help people effect personal growth/development in life and business. He is the founder, chairman, and president of OCP-IP and has served on the boards of various groups. Since 1980, he* *has held senior management positions in Silicon Valley with National Semiconductor, VLSI Technology (now NXP), PMC-Sierra, Mentor Graphics, and several start-up companies. He holds a master of science in microelectronics from Southampton University, England.*

Introduction

The Basics: What You Need to Do to Get the Job You Want

Whether you are a junior manager or a seasoned executive, it is certain you will benefit from optimizing the development of your foundational managerial skills. The purpose of this book is to help you with this process in the simplest and most efficient fashion possible. Again, this does not mean teaching you how to develop those skills; it means showing you how to assess yourself honestly and determine the needs of your targeted job, so that you can design an effective plan for your career, given the skills you already have. In other words, you will learn how to critically assess yourself so that you can present your skills to create your best-possible value, with the end goal of becoming the inevitable choice for the management position you desire.

This book will provide, in quick-read format, the empowering tools necessary to accurately assess your current skill level, determining your own mastery, adequacy, and deficiency accordingly, so that you can then target areas needing improvement and successfully develop simple follow-up plans to get the results you require.

Importantly, this process will ensure minimizing your investment while maximizing your return. Let's face it, if you can proactively, accurately, and efficiently target only the specific development you need, you can then ensure that you have the right skills in place to provide you the best shot to attain that management position you desire.

The information in subsequent sections precisely and concisely outlines and describes only the critical skills that should be of general concern to all managers (and that can equally apply to the self-employed). These skills and behaviors need not all be learned immediately by every manager. (Some managers won't ever need to learn all of them.) For this reason, they are presented in a fashion that permits you to easily assess what is important for you right now. Based on this rapid evaluation and self-assessment, you can then target the very best items to match your immediate development needs. This process ensures that you will avoid the traditionally wasteful, career-consuming, hit-and-miss approach, which involves reading random books, listening to irrelevant talks, and attending what can often turn out to be unnecessary seminars.

What's Next?

It's important that you enjoy this book and the process of self-development. Certainly, everything is presented and provided in the most concise fashion possible, distilled to only the most essential information that you can immediately use and apply to your own situation. To achieve this extremely concise form, much of this text is written in a compact, abbreviated style. This not only ensures the most efficient use of your time, it also enables you to quickly reread, reassess, and revisit any components that warrant your additional review.

Please be sure to read the next section, "How to Best Utilize This Book," before you start reading the individual sections.

How to Best Utilize This Book

Again, this book is designed to be a "go-to" quick reference that will help you assess and plan your course of action without wasting your time or energy. It will not teach you how to gain what you lack, but it will show you how to formulate an effective, streamlined plan to get the job you want.

I recommend that you read this book from start to finish, completing the total self-assessment after you have read the sections that define the fifteen essential managerial skills. (Alternatively, you may wish to simply look at the skills required for the job you desire, and then design your plan to ensure that you meet just those specific requirements. However, I believe it to be in your best interest to follow the entire process as described in this book, which will benefit you short- and long-term.)

Before you dive into the central sections, let's just briefly review the entire process of self-assessment and streamlined career planning:

- List the most significant skills and behaviors possessed by well-developed managers.

11

- Explain the specifics involved in mastering these skills (but it will not teach you how to develop the skills you lack).
- Help you determine your own strengths and weaknesses regarding these individual skills.
- Help you itemize those skills you should personally target in order to support your immediate growth and career needs.
- Help you design a self-development plan to target specific positions and manage progress along your chosen career path.
- Provide you with the ongoing ability to reassess and revisit your growth needs as they evolve in the future.

In other words, the total self-assessment will show you who you are in terms of your current skills. The review of the position you seek will show you which skills you need to have in order to get the job you want. The streamlined plan will provide you with a goal-oriented road map for getting the job you desire. This book is designed to be used throughout your career life—whether you work as an in-house manager ascending the corporate ladder or embark on self-employment.

Development is an ongoing process, and as you advance, your needs and goals will change. The best way to use this book is the one that most suits your objectives at any given time. Rest assured that the material will serve your development needs as they evolve, so long as you undertake with honesty and purpose all the activities outlined in the following pages.

To sum up, using the process of honest skill assessment and targeted planning described in this book will help you chart your course throughout your career by targeting the positions you desire and then proactively developing yourself and your skill set to match the positions you seek. As long as you complete the self-assessment honestly and revisit the process at different points in your life, this book will remain an invaluable objective guide throughout your ongoing journey.

Now all that remains is for you to dive in and take control of architecting and targeting your personalized career path. So, with my best wishes in hand, let the process begin ...

Part I

Understanding and Assessing Your Management Skills

Fifteen Essential Managerial Skills

So what is this skill set that we should consider and select from in order to pursue your personal development? Let's consider the following generic capabilities that an expert and competitively attractive management candidate should want to possess, understand, and have largely mastered:

1. Specific job-related skills and training*
2. Problem solving
3. Decision analysis
4. Interpersonal relationships/management styles
5. Delegating
6. Motivating
7. Planning
8. Organizing
9. Controlling
10. Reengineering
11. Team playing
12. Leading
13. Mentoring

---

* Be aware that this is profession specific, not generic, and as such, will be treated differently from the other essential skills, 2 through 15, inclusive.

14. Time management
15. Public speaking/presenting

How to Make the Most Effective Use of This List

Truly this is a formidable list, but what many of you will discover is that your skills are already quite sound or serviceable, good, or even excellent in any number of these competence areas, even if you have deficiencies requiring immediate improvement in other areas. Let me reemphasize once again that our aim is not to teach you how to gain or develop any or all of these skills, but to help you assess your current level of skills—mastery, adequacy, or deficiency. Thus, what we must quickly do is document that set of skills which is unique to you. Armed with this, you can then put a simple plan in place that recognizes deficiencies, earmarks development plans, and yet lets you immediately put from your mind those issues where you now know your skills are acceptable and can be leveraged as is, and also where you excel so that you can showcase your best talents. Our goal is to create a concise, reliable, and honest self-assessment that will enable you to formulate an effective and workable career/ personal development plan.

The elegance of this plan is its efficiency. No longer are you constrained by waiting for company training that may or may not be forthcoming; no longer do you have to wait and hope for a management position that may belatedly bring you the development skills you already need. Now you can also be free from canned schemes that address the needs of many but that are not personalized to your specific development needs. Remember that the information presented in the following sections will enable you to quickly recognize where you excel (mastery), where you are average (adequacy), and where you need to improve (deficiency). This will then allow you to select those elements that will best enhance your personal chances and your prominence in the eyes of those able to select you for that key management position you desire. After all, if you proactively demonstrate the skills of that next position or opportunity, who wouldn't choose you in order to assist with their own staffing situation or business needs?

So let us proceed. In the following sections we will look at each of the fifteen individual management skills listed above, briefly describe what they are, and provide you with the tools you need to assess your current level of capability. After this, we will help you prioritize the elements in a development plan. Moving forward, you can either select one or two higher elements of concern for your development, or lay out a complete long-term development plan that will carry you through for years. It is your own choice whether to work on a few immediate essentials, a long-term plan, or even a single item. Again, this gives you the ability to make the best use of your time, resources, and energy by streamlining your focus into an effective, realistic, goal-oriented purpose.

In the future, you may choose to redefine or revisit the road map for your personal development. You always have the opportunity to return to this reference material to reassess yourself in light of changed responsibilities, additional personal development, and anything else pertinent. In this way, you will always have a tool at the ready to reassess what you should focus upon next. The process is simple to follow and easy to repeat in the future.

The basic skill-set definitions for managers will change little over the years. You, however, will develop and enhance your own abilities as the weeks and years pass. Whatever competence level you attain in any specific management skill area, you can (and really should) always have a prioritized list of those elements you still want and/or need to enhance. Something you possess adequacy in now might require mastery in order to obtain the position you desire—or you might just need such mastery in the future, regardless—thus, awareness of your own skill set at any given moment is crucial to your success. So, at any critical time in your future, you can readily return to this reference material, reevaluate yourself, and quickly redefine the customized development in which you personally need to invest in order to ensure that you succeed in achieving your goals.

Key Points to Remember

This list of fifteen essential managerial skills is your starting point for self-development, as it shows you all the critical areas in which you need to effectively assess your current skills. After that, you can determine which of those critical areas are most important to the job you seek, and how much you need to improve in order to present yourself as the ideal candidate. Armed with all this, you can then craft a workable, streamlined self-development plan to meet your goals. It is crucial for your self-assessment to be 100 percent honest, so, for your own sake, please make sure it is exactly that. Remember, this book's twofold purpose is assessment and planning. So let's get to it by delving into the fifteen skills, one by one.

Specific Job-Related Skills and Training

This particular section of skills is different from all others we will consider. All those skills described following this one (as listed 2 through 15, inclusive, on page 17 in "Fifteen Essential Managerial Skills") are generic management capabilities that are typically relevant to *all* professions. This section alone, however, will discuss those capabilities (academic, professional, and task-related) that are specific to your particular professional situation. Accordingly, further on in this section, we will assess your career needs in regard to this type of profession-specific development, as this is crucial to do before we move forward to describe the fourteen generic management skills that apply across all industries. (Again, generic skills are items 2 through 15, inclusive, on page 17 in "Fifteen Essential Managerial Skills.")

Qualifications

Here, we are talking about "formal qualifications," where the subject is often inherently less subjective. For this reason, it is more relevant that we should now concern ourselves with the different situations in which you might find yourself; namely, when specific (usually "academic") qualifications are well defined and required, and, conversely, when they are not. Let us now tackle the subject in just those classifications, consider some more general matters, and then contemplate the scenarios where a change of venue might be appropriate, given the circumstances and requirements of your targeted employment for these specific qualifications, job-related skills, and training.

In reality, there is generally not much material offering guidance that helps you find your way through the maze of required (and "possibly required") qualifications for your target position. So let's proceed with a short discussion and see if we can proffer some valuable advice and insights.

When Qualifications Are Well Defined

There are obvious cases, such as a CTO position, where responsibilities may be somewhat unambiguous, and, say, perhaps a PhD in a specific discipline or field is "expected." You must recognize such firm requirements for the job you seek, and then either bite the bullet to comply or move on to an adjacent role or situation more suitable for what you are prepared and able to invest.

If the barrier for entry is high and requires a significant investment on your part, you should be very certain that the time you invest will pay off. Also, there is not much point chasing an advanced qualification for a very specific position that may not even come free in the foreseeable future, unless there are alternative and viable career options in the same general direction to which such an investment can alternatively lead.

Where you have already met the requirements for your target position, you should additionally highlight any even vaguely appropriate special studies, personal interests, and pursuits that enhance your candidacy. Make sure such advantages are visible. If the target role could benefit from skills or talents not "required," but still clearly bringing great value, make sure you develop and/or promote your talent in those areas, too. This could be having fund-raising skills, for example, or any superior and specific management skills not previously expected, but which can offer clear and real advantages when accompanying a new appointee. There are plenty of such skills to consider; many are highlighted in this book!

When Qualifications Are Loosely Defined

In many professional settings, perhaps just a university degree is expected. However, the discipline for that degree is not always fixed. For example, consider a marketing role where degrees in business might be typically expected, but appointments can be common with general arts or even science-based qualifications. Sometimes such diversity is even welcomed when the candidate additionally possesses sufficient experience, some advanced skills, and a proven track record.

So your objective is to clearly understand where the bar is set, and then to be sure that the requirements are under your control and match what you can—or will—offer. Again, where a candidacy can benefit from skills or talents not formally specified, pick a winner, develop yourself in that skill, and be sure the result is visible and acknowledged.

General Tips

You should always be looking for ways to increase your value for your target role. Consider professional memberships (chartered engineer, fellowship in some organization, etc.) that might bring you an edge or even be an unstated "requirement" or preference.

Look to academic advances that can set you apart; perhaps an MBA is in order. Similarly, just simple study classes in an appropriate field can enhance your cause and bring value to your candidacy. Maybe you should take a simple accounting class where you are targeting a business position that would benefit from preexisting and tangible P&L exposure. The same might also be achieved by visibly boning up on appropriate materials that are willingly shared by a trained colleague.

Even companies that invest little in promoting self-development will often offer time off and tuition reimbursement to support self-motivated employees. Taking such initiative is often inherently well received, highly regarded, and, importantly, very visible.

The foregoing suggestions offer ways of adding value to your candidacy for that position you are targeting. The only limit to your self-development is your lack of willingness to do everything in your power to attain your goals.

Change of Venue

When we target careers, it is sometimes inevitable that success will move us outside our current groups, divisions, and even companies. Thus, some of our self-development should be highly promoted, whereas other improvements are better only displayed for the right "target audience." There is not much point in advertising and promoting those skills we are clearly developing for application blatantly outside the realm of our internally perceived career path!

Life is inherently simpler if your skills allow you to target and evolve a career within one company, but it is now well accepted that almost every professional will make five to ten fundamental lifetime career changes. As switching teams, and even disciplines, is somewhat inevitable, it is always wise to keep an open mind and selectively develop generic skills that can be leveraged outside even the most optimally planned career path.

Having a road map for your general skill set is certainly wise. Similarly, having a "skill map" for your career path is essential. Having both of these plans enables you to better select personal development that is foundationally strong so that it will remain in play as a lifelong investment that wasn't wasted.

Lastly, always remember that well-chosen, visible skills developed and behaviors learned simultaneously provide another qualification for the right target position!

Assessing Your Current Qualifications

We now need for you to consider a target job, or your career path in general, and then identify the specific job-related skills and training you should consider. To help you with this process, see Table X below, which is an example of items that might be completed.

**Table X: Example of Specific Job-Related
Skills and Training for Target Position**

WHAT'S NEEDED	START Date	COMPLETE Date
Academic		
Bachelor's		
MBA		
Master's (other than MBA)		
Doctorate		

Professional Designations/Memberships
C. Eng. Certification
Toastmasters
Fellowship
Task-Related Classes/Courses
Financial Statements
C++
PowerPoint
Excel
Foreign Language

Now, based on the example provided above in Table X, use the blank version provided in Table Y to fill in your own specific job-related skills and training for your targeted position.

Table Y: Your Specific Job-Related Skills and Training for Target Position

WHAT'S NEEDED	START Date	COMPLETE Date
Academic		

Professional Designations/Memberships

Task-Related Classes/Courses

You should develop this skill acquisition plan for each and every individual position you consider. This will fit conveniently into the timelines you need, or it will not. All that remains now is for you to commit to making the investments where you are deficient; if you would rather not, you should reconsider your career road map.

However, if you do already have the formal qualifications that will be required, you are truly home free; if you excel in any area that is necessary for the targeted position, even better!

Reference Materials

Specific reference materials are not really relevant to this subject area. In this matter, the first part of the background information you need to ascertain is obtained by bluntly (or discreetly, as the case may be) asking an HR person (or another trusted colleague) to advise you of the particular qualifications required for the position that interests you. The second part of the equation is for you to determine (or assess) what other skills you might bring to the table that would best further your personal cause to be promoted into that position. What skills and value can you bring, ahead of others, that will make you the most suitable and likely candidate for that targeted position?

It is worth mentioning that significant up-front care should be taken to avoid any ambiguity regarding qualifications and skills required to secure a particular position. Avoid misunderstandings early on, as they can have catastrophic downstream impacts upon your long-term career planning!

Key Points to Remember

Qualifications, whether formally specified or loosely defined, are integral to selecting the ideal candidate. An honest self-assessment of your existing skills (Table Y) in relation to the qualifications of the position you seek is critical to *your* selection as that ideal candidate. Resist the temptation to sugarcoat your skills and experience; be clear and direct, and streamline your plan to develop and/or showcase your best features and compensate for your worst.

Problem Solving

The Importance of Problem Solving

Problem solving is one of the hardest skills to present in a concise form, and in turn, to permit a simple self-assessment (decision analysis, reviewed in the next section, is equally difficult in this regard). It is a tough subject to learn without taking a class, and few strong written materials are available on the topic, which makes its description even more difficult. Nevertheless, problem solving is a critical management skill, fundamental to improving businesses and to rectifying and/or effectively evolving any less-than-optimal situations.

Ideally, on a day-to-day basis, managers spend most of their time working on routine matters that they (or others) have already controlled within an optimized process, or on other items that they personally need to execute rather than delegate. A good percentage of their remaining time should then best be utilized in focusing upon improvements. That means fixing things that are broken and/or improving current systems and situations; in short, problem solving.

Whether we are routinely processing information, installing new processes, or making repairs, we are always engaged in some form of problem solving. Inevitably, the better you are at solving problems, the more value you can bring to the table. So it is worth quickly reviewing the process, actions, and behaviors described below. Once having reviewed that, you will be able to assess your own current capabilities and determine any relevant need for improvement with respect to that management role you seek.

Remember, this book will not teach you how to develop this skill; it will merely highlight the importance of problem solving, provide a concise summary of it, and then enable you to assess your current skill level and design your plan accordingly.

What Is Problem Solving?

Problem solving is about process and organization. Clear thinking is always important, but if you understand how to systematically and repeatedly gather information about any new problem you encounter, you will invariably succeed in solving that problem. Again, high achievers are often skilled problem solvers. It should be noted, however, that this is not because of a high IQ or some special gift; rather, it is because such individuals are specifically trained in the skill (or well-read on the subject, adequately mentored, or previously exposed by direct experience). Alternatively, they may be sufficiently analytical by nature to unwittingly process information in much the same manner as described below, which enables them to excel as problem solvers.

Humans are natural problem solvers, but the vast majority of the challenges we address are trivial, direct, and cause-and-effect in nature. When answers and underlying problems are less obvious, a true skill set and a well-proven process is essential. This means that when things do become obscure, difficult, and complex, we'd be wise to already have established tools and training in our personal arsenal.

Problem-solving enterprises can vary from solitary exercises to team processes. Sometimes these go even further, requiring the prominent leadership of teams, becoming so-called "task forces." Therefore, if you need to improve your value by being seen as a strong leader, a problem solver, and a can-do individual, your best opportunity to do so is by solving problems *and* getting results. Problem solving is not just an essential management skill; it is a core competence for managers and leaders. Any manager will always benefit from establishing a strong initial competence in this area, or from at least improving the skill to become as competent as possible.

Overview of Training and Tools

Those books and materials available generally segment the description of this skill into six areas. Typically, the segmentation of those areas can be split up in different ways, but they will always explain a method for developing and practicing problem-solving skills. In general, the skill set and methods are quite simple to understand and learn. This is fortunate, as our individual ability to maximize problem-solving skills is not only a managerial asset but also an invaluable personal advantage in day-to-day living.

Effective training and tools should include the behaviors and practices described below. Let's outline them so that you can more easily determine whether you need to further develop this skill. (Again, the aim is not to teach you this skill, but rather to provide a sufficient summary to enable you to assess yourself and plan your self-development accordingly.)

Case Histories
Firstly, it is important that you study **case histories.** These highlight and demonstrate the criticality of this skill, while also

providing working examples that you can use to explore as you practice the behavior. Problem solving has obvious uses in such areas as manufacturing, operations, and research, but it has equal value in improving and/or fixing sales, marketing, and even HR issues. Its application is both diverse and powerful. Problem solving is a core skill for those who lead others, as unsolved problems leave residual liabilities, including unnecessary costs, poor quality, and unreliable yields and outcomes. Companies have literally gone out of business because of their failure to correctly analyze the root causes of problems and implement adequate corrective actions.

Symptoms of the Problem

When something needs to be fixed or seriously improved, the first order of business is to define and list those issues observed. Next, you must identify the **symptoms of the problem**. We need to record *what* these symptoms are, *when* they occur, and *where* and the *extent* to which we observe them. The basic idea is that we classify the symptoms so that we might compare potential root causes (i.e., "problems") linked to the information we have recorded in these classifications. This codification of the problems is shown in Table 1, below. Note that we are seeking to classify not only *what, when, where,* and to which *extent* we observe the symptom, but also to identify *what, when, where,* and to which *extent* we **do not** observe that symptom. This will help us comprehensively delineate and record what can sometimes be an overwhelming set of information that we need to categorize and consider when reviewing possible root causes and comparing them to a completed list of these symptoms.

Table 1: Codification of Problems

	IS the problem	Is NOT the problem
What		
When		
Where		
Extent		

Recording the Facts

Next, you must begin **recording the facts**. In this key step of the problem-solving process, you will take the format of Table 1 and simply make a chart. This may be on a single sheet of paper or on your computer screen if you are working alone, or on a large board or display screen if you are working with an extensive team or many participants. Basically the chart, with its four rows for symptoms, needs to be loaded with the factual data of those observations that you have made regarding the problem. You will record entries that correspond to the *what, when, where,* and *extent* lines of Table 1. Similarly, and also following Table 1, you will need to recognize when the symptom *is* or *is not* contributing to the problem, and then document an explicit record in the corresponding column. The idea is to gather up all the facts and observations and then load that data into your chart. All data should be accounted for and recorded, regardless of its initially perceived importance (or insignificance), as it may ultimately prove valuable in validating the nature of the ultimate root cause of the problem, or in just eliminating potential theories already proven wrong from repeated future consideration that wastes time and effort.

Brainstorming Root Causes

After you have a record of all the facts and observations about the problem, you must begin **brainstorming root causes** (of problems). This can be a solitary event if you're working alone, or an opportunity for a team (or even multiple teams) to attack the problem from different directions. It's usually best that a unified group of diverse background disciplines comes together to suggest potential root causes. When brainstorming, you should leverage group dynamics and stimulate ideas for the most diverse possibilities. Potential root causes should come from insightful, closely involved individuals, as well as from casual observers who offer a unique and even divergent perspective. It is essential that root causes represent ideas "from the sublime to the ridiculous." The most slightly suspected or unlikely suggestion can be quickly eliminated when played against the record of the facts (gathered in Table 1, above). This exercise should truly be brainstorming: just put together a list of ideas without overanalyzing them. Reviewing these ideas for credibility is a separate and subsequent phase in the process. At the end of this phase you will have a simple list of potential root causes.

Evaluating the Possibilities

Next, you must begin **evaluating the possibilities**. You simply take each potential root cause, one at a time, and check it against the completed list of known facts (Table 1, with all observations and data inserted). Root causes that don't fit the facts can simply be eliminated and never discussed again. All such eliminated root causes should be crossed out, but keep them on the list. Any additional data garnered during this process should be added to the record of tabulated facts, as appropriate. You will continue refining and reviewing root causes until one fits the complete record of facts that you have assembled.

It is essential that once the root cause (problem) is determined, it should then be proven and validated by devising a simple test (or tests) that unambiguously substantiates its selection.

Installing Solutions

Lastly, you must begin **installing solutions**. Corrective actions must be taken to attack the root causes that resulted in the observations of the problem. You do not want to merely fix symptoms; whenever possible and practical, you want to correct the real root cause(s). So we must verify potential fixes, document them, and then install processes to ensure their secure, ongoing success. It is important to broadcast problems and solutions outside of the immediate group involved with their correction. This not only promotes the team and its success, but it is also great for morale and highlights the value of problem solving for potential reuse and application elsewhere. In many cases, perhaps the most important contribution to make is in installing (or recommending) the practice of problem solving more broadly across the organization.

The steps outlined above provide a very brief overview of the problem-solving process, designed and provided for the economic use of your time. Writers and trainers in this area prepare and offer exhaustive explanations of the reasons and thinking that are involved in this process. These are described here only cursorily, in simple sentences and phrases, as this book does not aim to teach you how to develop management skills. The purpose of the above overview is to help you understand what is generally involved in problem-solving skills and behaviors.

Problem solving is an organized process, and it is important that you recognize it as such. Like many skills, merely reading about problem solving is not as potent for your development as being in an environment where you actually practice the behavior. Such skills are always highly valued within all organizations, and any success in practicing such skills on a visible project can indeed be instrumental in bringing exciting and interesting benefits to your career. The outline of the process provided above should help you assess if problem solving is an important, critical, or essential skill for you to develop. It will also help you determine if you are utilizing effective training and tools.

Do You Possess Problem-Solving Skills?

It's usually pretty easy to tell. Just run through the bolded items above (under "Overview of Training and Tools"), and it should be clear. You are a person who is routinely finding obstacles and overcoming them quickly, or you are not. You frequently run into large problems that need to be analyzed and repaired with corrective action, or you do not. You will need to demonstrate such skills strongly and continually in your next role, or you will not. The issue becomes simply this: either you are currently sufficiently practiced in and adept at problem solving, or you already recognize some deficiencies that you must address.

So, if you are not someone who quickly recognizes problems and is able to take action in an appropriate and organized fashion, you may need some work and self-development in this area. Additionally, it is important for you to be able to address problems, not just when you are working alone but also when you are working within a group setting. If you suffer any confidence or skill issues in leading groups in this way, actually practicing and developing your problem-solving techniques in a more organized and formal setting would be very appropriate and helpful for you in your goal of attaining the management position you desire. Clearly, like many skills, problem solving needs to be practiced within the context of a broader set of personal capabilities as well. (This broader set would include leading groups, motivating others, etc.—*see* the "Fifteen Essential Managerial Skills," page 17).

Assessing Your Current Skill Level

Just score yourself excellent (E), average (A), or poor (P) in the total set of behaviors and practices described above (bolded items under "Overview of Training and Tools"), and then keep a record of your single score in the skill of problem solving by making a note on Table 6A in part II, page 142. We will assess later if this should be a priority self-development area for you.

Reference Materials

Having read the descriptions of processes and practices above, you may find that you are missing personal and unique behaviors that are clearly essential to augment important, but more minor, aspects of your skill set in this area. If this is the case, rather than seeking traditional and "complete" written materials (books and pamphlets, etc.) or a canned course, your development might best be facilitated through mentoring, or perhaps by seeking more customized training through personal contacts who can offer such special content arrangements and guidance.

Online you will find a number of tools available, including websites offering various resources on the subject, as well as a number of classes and courses. Resources tied to scientific method are generally of particular value. Basic online search terms suffice, such as *problem solving* and *problem-solving skills.*

A body of work exists that discusses and bemoans the fundamental lack of tools routinely available to business managers and featured in academic training. Be sure to select adequately business-centric materials that provide sufficiently in-depth coverage, matching just your own development needs and little more.

Key Points to Remember

Problem solving is a core competence for all managers and a critical business skill. In addition, it is important for daily life! If you possess this key skill, you will automatically present as a valuable candidate for any management position you seek. If you need development in this area, putting forth the effort will better help you meet your career goals.

Decision Analysis

The Importance of Decision Analysis

A few written materials (particularly books) are available in this area, but the subject matter tends to better lend itself to face-to-face instruction. In fact, it is tough to learn decision analysis (DA) without taking a class. In addition, it is one of the hardest skills to describe in a concise form, and thereby to permit a simple self-assessment (problem solving, reviewed in the previous section, is equally difficult in this regard). Inevitably, because DA is such a key, higher-value skill, it requires a larger investment of time and effort. The ability to make crisp decisions is certainly a highly valued management skill. Indeed, this skill is truly valuable for both one's personal and professional life.

Like many skills, DA is highly process-centric. So let's review this process and proceed to evaluate your need for personal improvement. However, remember that this book will not teach you this skill; it will merely highlight the importance of DA, provide a concise summary of it, and then empower you to assess your current skill level and design your plan accordingly.

What Is Decision Analysis?

DA is about making the best-available choice, when a selection is required. It is often the case that managers and individuals get caught up with emotional needs and preferences that are narrow-minded or simply not sufficiently objective. Most of the time, it is easy for us to step back and make an objective call, but when the alternatives are numerous and complex, and/or the decision is weighty, it is better to have an objective process that clarifies the real issues and makes certain we secure the best choice from among all those options. Furthermore, it is also the case that any manager needing to "play Solomon" and "make the right choice" certainly needs a tool at his or her disposal that will visibly ensure the demonstration of detached and logical thinking, reliably secure buy-in from a group of (perhaps fractious) stakeholders, and leave in place a relatively indisputable result that everyone can logically accept and trust. Again, the ability to achieve such results is a clearly critical skill.

Overview of Training and Tools

Most training materials and tools offer a multipart process: a two-part process that sets the stage, followed by a five-part process for systematically making a "best choice." As always, the descriptions may vary, but they will—and should—begin with largely the same overall approach.

Effective training and tools should include the behaviors and practices described below. Let's outline them so that you can more easily determine whether you need to further develop this skill. (Again, the aim is not to teach you this skill, but rather to provide a sufficient summary to enable you to assess yourself and plan your self-development accordingly.)

Remaining Objective

Firstly, **remaining objective** is critical. It is essential to let agreed-upon facts dictate the final result, but with the understanding that best choices are not always overwhelmingly perfect. Indeed, in complex situations we are often destined to find only "the best choice" for the currently understood situation and circumstances. Above all else, we must prevent emotion and bias from ultimately affecting the selection process. This also means that we must follow a process and make speedy selections.

Acting as a Team

Secondly, although this entire process can be performed by an individual alone, throughout this discussion we will consider the situation and importance of **acting as a team.** When operating with a team, we must first pick someone to drive the process. The leader should move quickly, not bias voting or scoring, and generally be perceived as neutral and systematic in this role. When we ultimately derive a result, it must be publically acknowledged, so as to (1) avoid fallbacks and revisits of the process (unless there are profound changes or understanding of facts that should be considered), *and* (2) get everyone on board.

Remaining objective and acting as a team sets the stage (two-part process referred to above). Once the ground rules are set, we should consider the process of systematically making the decision (five-part process referred to above).

Deriving the Selection Criteria

First in the actual decision process is **deriving the selection criteria**. This is the selection of those factors against which we will evaluate the choices we have. We begin by making a list of all these elements that can reasonably be considered by the team. These factors can be measurable hard criteria or even soft/subjective requirements (*see* Table 2, below). What is important is that this list is objectively compared individually against "seriousness," "urgency," and "impact on long-term growth," in order to derive the ranked order of their importance. It is important that the ranking of these criteria is performed by the team, which will assess each factor as a high (H), medium (M), or low (L) score against "seriousness, "urgency," etc., in turn.

Table 2: Example Ranking for Random Selection Criteria

Impact on Selection Criteria	Seriousness	Urgency	Long-Term Growth
Resale Price	H (3)	M (2)	H (3)
Flexibility	M (2)	L (1)	L (1)
Color selection	H (2)	L (1)	H (3)
Cost	H (3)	H (3)	H (3)
Performance	M (2)	M (2)	H (3)

[**NOTE:** *For convenience, when there are many selection criteria, high, medium, and low rankings can be converted to actual scores (H = 3, M = 2, L = 1, as shown, above).*]

Now that we have a ranked assessment for our example criteria, we can put them in order of importance and afford them individual ratings or "weights." This is shown in Table 3, below.

Table 3: Example of Random Criteria in Ranked Order and with Weights of Importance

Selection criteria	Weight
Cost (9)	5
Resale price (8)	4
Performance (7)	3
Color (6)	2
Flexibility (4)	1
[NOTE: Table 3 illustrates an example of random criteria placed in ranked order with derived "weights" of importance. If there are five criteria, weights run 1 through 5, and so on.]	

Listing the Choices

The second step in implementing our decision process is **listing the choices.** Here, the team can brainstorm a list of alternatives that are viable selections for our decision analysis. It is important that all participants have a relatively common and shared understanding of each of these choices. Certainly, there must be knowledge within the team that ensures each of the choices can be accurately evaluated against every selection criteria already defined, ranked, and weighted (per the process outlined above). In order to move our working example forward as efficiently as possible, let us consider that we have choices 1, 2, and 3.

Evaluating the Choices versus the Selection Criteria

Next in our process is **evaluating the choices versus the selection criteria**. We now consider our choices valued against the selection criteria, and then we score them accordingly. The simple example of such processing appears and is continued in Table 4, below. It is important that each choice is valued in turn against each selection criteria, one at a time. Once this is done, we can proceed to the next selection criteria, and so on. Scoring is always on a scale of 1 to 10, with 10 being the best (maximum) score. The best choice receives the maximum score, and the next-best choice is scored relatively. Table 4 also illustrates this important differentiation.

Table 4: Example of Available Choices
Evaluated against Selection Criteria

	Cost	Resale	Performance	Color	Flexibility
	(5)	(4)	(3)	(2)	(1)
Choice 1	10	10	5	9	10
Choice 2	8	9	10	10	6
Choice 3	2	8	9	6	9

If we now take the *products* for the score of each choice multiplied by the weight of each of the selection criteria, we have our final assessment, as illustrated in Table 5, below.

Table 5: Example of Final Assessment of Choices

	Cost	Resale	Performance	Color	Flexibility	TOTAL SCORE
	(5)	(4)	(3)	(2)	(1)	
Choice 1	50	40	15	18	10	133
Choice 2	40	36	30	20	6	132
Choice 3	10	32	27	12	9	90

[**NOTE:** *Table 5 illustrates the actual scores achieved by the choices available as influenced (multiplied) by the selection criteria.*]

Measuring the Result

The fourth step in the process is **measuring the result**. For convenience, our simple example already has the total score shown in Table 5, above. The importance of this step is that we take these results literally. In the case where our results are almost identical (as in a simple example), we could take either choice 1 or choice 2 as the best selection; clearly, they both are superior to choice 3. On the rare occasions where scores come out so close together, we have the option to toss a coin, choose that which is most popular, or indeed allow the ultimate decision maker to pick between those two tied choices with little fear of group criticism! Once the process is complete, it is essential that we stop talking about those choices that have been clearly eliminated and that we move on with plans that support the primary choice.

Sticking with the Decision

The fifth and final step in this process is **sticking with the decision**. Sometimes, we may have selection criteria that are a "must." This means that any final choice has to satisfy the criteria; otherwise, it is not viable. For example, it might be that the cost of our final choice cannot exceed, say, *x* dollars. Any choice that does not pass such specific criteria must be eliminated from the selection process early on and not discussed further; it is simply not a valid option. In completing our process, we must communicate its result to all affected or concerned, and if necessary, display the logical process by which the ultimate selection was made. Thereafter, all involved should walk in lockstep in support of the decision.

The above overview is, within itself, quite definitive. Certainly, with this basic introduction, even someone never previously exposed to this methodology or process should be capable of performing a decision analysis. In this case, perhaps more than most, "practice does make perfect," and the subtleties of this skill and process are certainly enhanced by both formal training and individual practice. Many questions cannot be answered here in this simple, abbreviated explanation of the behavior and skill set. I'm sure many readers may now be motivated to further study and answer the questions inevitably raised in their minds as they walked through this description and accompanying example. Truly, DA training is a major enhancement of any manager's skill set. It's hard to believe any management professional will not benefit by investing significant time and energy into formal development of this powerful tool.

Do You Possess Decision-Analysis Skills?

It is simple for you to understand whether you have the skill to run this process. You already know if you've had the formal training to use this tool. You will also be able to recall if you have needed to use such a process in the past, just as you should be able to deduce whether this would be of value to you in any future management position, particularly your target position.

In any event, you should run through the bolded items above (under "Overview of Training and Tools"), and it should be relatively clear. See if this general description provides you sufficient personal information and confidence to at least practice the process in private. Perhaps this description is sufficient to develop the skill on personal issues and matters. You can then apply the skill to workplace situations as you feel sufficiently confident to do so. However, consider this caveat: if you plan on bypassing more formal training and, instead, leveraging the simple introduction provided above, just be sure you're well practiced and confident with the process before you display your DA prowess in the workplace. Again, remember that we have covered only an outline of the process. Studying the actual skill is more complicated, and you would be well advised to take a class if you are unsure of your DA skills.

Assessing Your Current Skill Level

Just score yourself excellent (E), average (A), or poor (P) in the total set of behaviors and practices described above (bolded items under "Overview of Training and Tools"), and then keep a record of your single score in the skill of decision analysis by making a note on Table 6A in part II, page 142. We will assess later if this should be a priority self-development area for you.

Reference Materials

A particularly diverse set of websites, portals, journals, books, tools, articles, training, and even membership societies can be found online. The description provided above (under "Overview of Training and Tools") offers the outline of a personally preferred methodology and process. This subject is particularly suitable for a class or course, especially if it is combined with problem solving.

Useful search terms include *decision analysis, management decision tools, decision-making techniques,* and *decision-making methods.*

If, upon further review of the reference materials, you recognize that this is a particularly necessary development area, and/or if your current skills are rather light, some form of a training class is strongly recommended. I simply cannot overemphasize the criticality of this fundamental managerial skill!

Key Points to Remember

Decision analysis (DA), like problem solving, is foundational to all management positions. Display of this skill will surely add value to your candidacy for your target job—and for any managerial job—so it can only be to your advantage to master this skill. Be sure to carefully consider taking a class or formal training in DA if you feel your skills are less than optimal.

Interpersonal Relationships/ Management Styles

The Importance of Interpersonal Relationships and Management Styles

This topic is referred to by a variety of terms, including *interpersonal relationships, management styles, interpersonal communications, personality types,* or even variations thereof. Here, we will use **interpersonal relationships** and **management styles** interchangeably for the purpose of outlining the skill set. Once again, remember that this book will not teach you this skill; it will merely highlight the importance of interpersonal relationships and management styles, provide a concise summary of them, and then empower you to assess your current skill level and design your plan accordingly.

This area also tends to be a little different from many other disciplines and skills covered in this text. Much of the information available on this subject is usually not readily and effectively self-administered by reading books. Generally, the most wholesome development is obtained by attending any of the numerous courses offered. Attendance is normally preceded by the completion of questionnaires: usually by yourself, your coworkers, and a supervisor.

Those materials provided commercially are generally offered by "training companies" that base their wares on the expert study of developers who have often spent many years characterizing and then codifying personality types.

Unfortunately, classes on managing interpersonal relationships, or management styles, are often, though not always, offered as a result of on-the-job issues that are already visible. As a result, it's better not to wait on this subject, but rather to be proactive in your personal development. Most people who have undergone such training will relate that once the subject is methodically studied, the differences discovered in people's personalities (or "styles") often prove quite shocking. Indeed, the first exposure to this technology is quite an eye-opener!

What Are Interpersonal Relationships and Management Styles?

This subject is about understanding the codification of personality or management styles, recognizing those different types, and adapting oneself to optimize interpersonal communications. Questionnaires (typically deployed as a precursor to understanding your own style) will undertake to characterize your style by considering such factors as individual focus on results, activities, relationships, systems, etc., as well as individual propensity for analysis, control, extroversion (or introversion), ability to empathize, etc.

I have seen the whole spectrum of differing management styles pigeonholed in as few as eight classifications (typically, in a matrix format). Similarly, I have seen as many as sixty-four (and heard of more!) presented by different training companies to represent the entire range of what can be considered to represent all personality types. Whether eight, sixty-four, or even more variations are offered is not important. Certainly, the purpose of the training is to show you where *you* are positioned, to offer a range of possible variations, and to better help you understand how to relate to those different styles.

Better understanding where your style fits in any group of characteristics helps you better understand where others fit and how they differ; as a result, you can learn to make the adjustments that will best help you to work effectively with such individuals. So you must identify and accept yourself in the landscape of styles that exist, and then you must develop the skills (based on the prescribed characteristics promoted in the course) to modify your behavior and make yourself a successful communicator "free of interpersonal relationship problems"!

Even if you are already considered skilled in working with others, formal training will quite often further enhance your abilities in this area and prepare you for future situations. Inevitably, you will run into problematic relationship issues in the workplace in the future, even if you have no such current challenges. Certainly, if you are lacking in this area it is a skill set you should immediately consider mandatory for development in order to make any progress in a management career.

Overview of Training and Tools

Typically, most training materials will describe the subject by considering six areas. These may be grouped, ordered, or presented in different ways, but they will invariably march you through the same set of experiences. Effective training and tools should include the behaviors and practices described below. Let's outline them so that you can more easily determine whether you need to further develop this skill. (Again, the aim is not to teach you this skill, but rather to provide a sufficient summary to enable you to assess yourself and plan your self-development accordingly.)

Completing Forms and Questionnaires

Firstly is the inevitable step of **completing forms and questionnaires**. Often, four or more colleagues will answer extensive questions about their observations of your style and behaviors. Similarly, you will make your own submission of replies that explore your likes, dislikes, and general tendencies in different situations. The resulting data is submitted to reviewers (normally computerized), which enables them to identify (as essential groundwork) the basic management style of those contributors. With this essential groundwork, they can then pinpoint your particular style (or pigeonhole you) in their particular scheme of categorizations. So you are now identified in a particular "management style."

Reviewing the Results

Our next step is **reviewing the results**. Sometime after all the forms and questionnaires have been completed and submitted, you will see the resulting analysis. (Generally, this takes a week or two, but you may receive the analysis almost immediately if you opt for an online offering as opposed to attending a formal class.) You are now placed in your specific pigeonhole, based on the characteristics and interests explored in the questionnaire (i.e., your focus on results or systems, interest in analysis, need for control, ability to empathize, etc.). Often, you will be told which well-known public figures share your specific personal profile. This has the dual benefit of making you more comfortable with the analysis of yourself and more receptive to positively accepting who you are and moving forward with the process.

Understanding Your Own Management Style

Now that you have a defined (or codified) personality, you move to the next step: **understanding your own management style**. Your specific style/profile is explained with respect to the data gathered— your strengths, your weaknesses, the dominant tendencies for your style in different situations, and so on. It is always explained that no style is "bad" or "good"; rather, it is your ability to adapt and work with others that is key. Suggestions are often offered on how to capitalize on your strengths and avoid your personal-style liabilities.

Understanding the Variety of Other Personality Types

Once you're schooled in the description of who you are, you reach the next important step: **understanding the variety of other personality types**. Having understood and codified your own style, you can now see the broad matrix of variations that identify each of the other possible styles. Time is then spent reviewing basic styles or major groupings of styles, the tendencies such people will demonstrate, and the generic needs they have in dealing and communicating effectively with others. You are now learning to recognize the key characteristics of other personality styles.

Reviewing How Your Style Relates to Others

The fifth element of training is generally **reviewing how your style relates to others**. Once you have located your place in the matrix of personality types and can identify those of others, you can then explore how to adapt your behavior to best communicate with those other types. You learn what to adapt in your behavior in order to better relate to other styles. Your ability to adapt seamlessly across many styles will determine your success as a communicator and manager. Importance will be placed upon your "flexibility" in dealing with, adapting to, and communicating with others.

Practicing a Problem or Example Case

The final portion of such trainings is typically **practicing a problem or example case**. Invariably, such classes offer you the chance to identify and answer questions about a "problem individual"; this could be a peer, a subordinate, your supervisor, or even a relative.

This person is classified for you by personality type, and you will be offered suggestions on how to work with that style, or be able to use this working example to practice your skills, in class and away from the "problem individual." If nothing else, such training will allow you some real guidance on improving upon at least one immediate and problematic relationship while you are actually in training! (Often this practice example will be initially developed by you ahead of the class, generally while completing the required forms and questionnaire.)

The above overview is certainly very brief, and it is designed and provided for the economic use of your time. Those effective writers and trainers in this area prepare and offer exhaustive descriptions detailing all the elements, personality types, and classification characteristics that are described here only cursorily. Materials available can help you comprehensively explore all the individual elements described above, and more, and also assist you with practices to follow in your office or workplace when managing interpersonal relationships with others. The important issue to grasp is understanding your own management style and how it can, and should, relate to others.

One last word about training in this particular area. Having been fortunate to attend a number of these classes over the years, I should add that the subject neither seemed repetitious upon revisiting, nor anything but a good investment of my time. This remained true whether the course was completed with peers, colleagues, or random individuals previously unknown to me.

Do You Have Effective Interpersonal Relationships? Do You Possess an Effective Management Style?

It's usually, but *not always,* pretty easy to tell. Just run through the bolded items above (under "Overview of Training and Tools"), and see if it's clear to you. Generally, if you have challenging relationships with one or more individuals, you will be aware of the problem. Somewhat of a concern should be the fact that problem relationships are often not apparent. Sometimes, particularly with subordinates, an individual may have a major issue working with your management style, and yet he or she will choose not to be open about the fact. In such cases, problems might be reported to "others," and this can serve as a background detractor to promotional opportunities that might otherwise have come your way.

If in doubt, you can always ask confidants who are prepared to share insights without that knowledge becoming broadly available. Certainly, you must reliably check how you are doing in the area of interpersonal relationships and then score yourself accordingly as to your need for personal development.

Assessing Your Current Skill Level

Just score yourself excellent (E), average (A), or poor (P) in the total set of behaviors and practices described above (bolded items under "Overview of Training and Tools"), and then keep a record of your single score in the skill of interpersonal relationships/management styles by making a note on Table 6A in part II, page 142. We will assess later if this should be a priority self-development area for you.

Reference Materials

As mentioned at the outset of this section, it is preferable—and, indeed, recommended—to complete a class or course in this subject area. Much can be discovered online as well, and this can serve as a basic introduction or a refresher, depending upon your specific situation.

Good search terms include *interpersonal relationships, management styles, interpersonal communications,* and *personality types.*

Key Points to Remember

Interpersonal skills are invaluable in business, regardless of your specific position. They are particularly crucial for managers. Understanding your own personality type (management style), as well as the personality types of others, will help you manage more effectively—and it is useful in day-to-day life as well. Displaying this skill will definitely enhance your candidacy for your target position.

Delegating

The Importance of Delegating

Delegating is essential to effective management, as the body of management literature will support. In fact, a lot of materials are available in this area, including a large number of capable and well-published authors and even several websites offering guidance. Many of the materials offered are centered on the basics and are ideal for more novice readers. Inevitably, no successful manager will travel very far up the food chain unless he or she can competently demonstrate the ability to delegate effectively. The skill of delegating is inherently tied to, and integrated with, both controlling and time management (each of which is covered separately later on in this book). So it is certainly worth quickly reviewing this discipline in order to assess your own current capabilities and needs for development and improvement. Let me reiterate that this book will not teach you this skill; it will merely highlight the importance of delegating, provide a concise summary of it, and then empower you to assess your current skill level and design your plan accordingly.

What Is Delegating?

Delegating is about achieving results through others. Again, if you are keenly sensitive to maximizing the use of your time and the results you achieve, you will be highly motivated to delegate effectively. Most high achievers will have figured out this opportunity and will thrive on any chance to leverage their influence by employing individuals and teams to accomplish their goals. Unfortunately, this by no means assures us that they will do this well, or with a motivating influence upon those who support them in their work. Similarly, there are those who are just not comfortable releasing the reins and empowering others, either because of their own insecurities or, perhaps, because of their basic lack of training in implementing this skill effectively. Whatever your own situation might be, find the opportunity to improve yourself in the execution of this critical set of behaviors.

Overview of Training and Tools

The description of this skill contains many nuances and individual pointers, and as such, it may be technically described in as many as a dozen "parts." (Eleven are outlined below.) These are often grouped in different ways, but the same issues are highlighted in most every description of the subject area. It is interesting that the most trivial pointers provided here can bring real value to even the most-experienced managers. You can learn from anywhere, and we all need refreshers, even if we are already beneficiaries of a lifetime of experience!

Effective training and tools should include the behaviors and practices described below. Let's outline them so that you can more easily determine whether you need to further develop this skill. (Again, the aim is not to teach you this skill, but rather to provide a sufficient summary to enable you to assess yourself and plan your self-development accordingly.)

Delegate or Die!

Firstly, you should recognize the need to **delegate or die**. It is important to learn to trust your direct reports and to rely on your own hiring choices and reviews. Leverage your perception of individuals, yet consider input provided on inherited employees. Be sure to give people the amount of rope they need to succeed, but not enough to hang themselves. Always think carefully about individuals' strengths and weaknesses, and build structures that will position them for success, accordingly. Remember, if you can't leverage the resources around you effectively by means of delegation, your organization will not accomplish essential and required results.

Effective Delegation Retains Control

The next critical thing to remember is that **effective delegation retains control**. You must utilize basic reviews of schedules and programs to keep things on track. Also, insert triggers that will highlight warning signs of problems. If employee weaknesses emerge, install support mechanisms and/or corrective actions to ensure their success and continued progress.

The Team Should Always Work Faster Than You Can Alone

Where delegation to more than one individual is involved, it is important to accept that **the team should always work faster than you can alone**. The team, as a group, will have better collective insight and often offer a superior view of alternatives. Empower the team and its leader. Clearly define and document goals and desired results. Be sure to allocate the essential resources—time, materials, manpower, etc.—that will ensure success.

Investing in the Kickoff

Before the action begins, you must **invest in the kickoff**. This is essential to provide guidance, insight, and any descriptions of available resources, etc., needed in order to fully commission the team (or individual). Make sure you identify your own availability to troubleshoot, provide guidance, and offer assistance so that momentum can be maintained. To expand upon a well-known analogy, teach folks to "fish" now, so you can benefit from their immediate results, long-term development, and motivated downstream contributions.

Establishing Commitment
Another up-front activity in delegation requires **establishing commitment**. Have both teams and individuals confirm that they understand the agreed-upon goals and objectives before they get under way. They should state this out loud to one another in your presence. Establish clear understandings before serious activity commences. Once on track, it may be difficult to make direction changes, so it is better if people are "bought in" and committed early on.

Extending Your Reach
Another goal of delegating is **extending your reach**. Well-delegated and properly monitored work magnifies your influence and the results you accomplish. Leveraging and empowering others through delegating frees you up to pursue different and more-challenging objectives personally, while simultaneously enabling you to continue to succeed in making broad-based accomplishments through your organization.

Empowering Others Grows Your Organization
Critical to your own success as a manager is understanding that **empowering others grows your organization**. This is another key goal of delegating, as successful teams thrive on well-managed responsibilities. The success of your employees reflects on you. Unless you are insecure as an individual, you should welcome sharing the successes of your team, even though the spotlight is

seemingly not on you, personally. Ultimately, the success of any team positively reflects on their management, and a successful team must be fully empowered so that they remain ready and willing to accomplish more.

Almost Everything Can Be Delegated

The wise manager understands that **almost everything can be delegated**. Take every opportunity to pass on tasks and programs to your team, wherever doing so is practical and/or can serve as a motivator. Keep only "must-do" work assignments, or politically sensitive projects, for yourself. Allow the projects and assignments to develop your staff. You should take these opportunities to grow your replacement in order to prudently enable and facilitate your own promotion.

Failure to Delegate Is Career Limiting

Remember that **failure to delegate is career limiting**. Not sharing interesting tasks and/or individual growth opportunities will "demotivate" employees. Managers who are slow to delegate inhibit the growth of teams and individuals, while at the same time visibly making themselves unfit for promotion. Be sure not to confine yourself with too many "individual projects," whereby you will be seen as someone who has reached a level where personal contributions are now overtaking your ability to work through others.

Celebrating Successes

Always important in delegating is **celebrating successes.** (This is equally important in motivating others, covered separately further on in this book.) When goals are achieved, ensure that personal and organizational acknowledgments occur and that rewards are plentiful and appropriate. Advise affected groups and people of new tools, practices, and/or procedures that affect workflows and interactions. If you are ever to err on praise, make sure it is by overkill; it is very unusual for people to *seriously* object to rewards or acknowledgments!

When Delegating Goes Wrong
We have seen all the ways for delegating to go right, but it can go wrong. You must be prepared for this too. We live and work in an imperfect world, and we may be required to react **when delegating goes wrong**. Always avoid blaming individuals, as it is generally rare for personnel to have acted maliciously. Similarly, take personal responsibility for your assignees and teams. Define and insert corrective action in a timely manner in order to leave everyone motivated to make progress, proceed, and act appropriately in the future. Above all else, be diplomatic and sensitive with redirects, reassignments, and corrective actions, but ***do not*** *ignore problems.* Understand and accept that, on some occasions, your own poor direction, control mechanisms, and/or monitoring may be the root of the problem. If so, accept, acknowledge, and learn.

Although very brief, the above overview still provides a fairly extensive review of the elements involved in practicing the skill of delegating. Presenters, authors, and trainers in this area may expand their description of individual details extensively; however, significantly, the bulk of learning and understanding available is mostly already contained in the precise review provided above. Again, it is important for you to go through the above description quickly, making a valid assessment of your own skills in the behavior of delegating and then determining if you need further development in this area.

Do You Possess Delegating Skills?

Here again, it's usually pretty easy to tell if you exhibit these behaviors. Just run through the bolded items above (under

"Overview of Training and Tools"), and it should be clear. You are handing out projects, commissioning teams, and initiating kickoffs, or you are not. Similarly, the teams are accomplishing their goals to agreed-upon standards, timelines, and costs, or they are not.

The reality for most managers is that their teams operate somewhere in between effectively and ineffectively. Assuming that you are not in a management position operating as an individual contributor and flirting with a status downgrade, your case is more likely to be one of a need for optimizing your delegating skills and practices. It is important to be clinically objective about how well you and your team(s) are doing, which will allow you to identify improvement opportunities for yourself and your team(s).

As always, it is wise to look to the future and assess the delegating skills you should ideally be demonstrating in order to make yourself the lead candidate for that next role you desire. Your current position may not fully provide the setting in which to best showcase your skills, but regardless of the situation, it's always in your best interest to highlight and prove your ability as an effective delegator and a manager able to achieve valuable results through others.

Assessing Your Current Skill Level

Just score yourself excellent (E), average (A), or poor (P) in the total set of behaviors and practices described above (bolded items under "Overview of Training and Tools"), and then keep a record of your single score in the skill of delegating by making a note on Table 6A in part II, page 142. We will assess later if this should be a priority self-development area for you.

Reference Materials

Introductory books on general management practices will provide further insights if the details provided above don't adequately suffice as basic introductions or refreshers. Online tools for training are available, along with other materials featured in the Free Management Library.

Useful search terms include *delegating, free management library,* and *management delegation.*

Key Points to Remember

Leveraging success through others—better known as delegating—is essential to effective management. Empowering your direct reports, individually and as a team, will show you to be a competent manager and leader. Visibly acknowledge and reward team successes, and you will showcase yourself as the lead contender for the promotion you desire.

Motivating

The Importance of Motivation

Much is offered in terms of training and materials in this management discipline. Like many of the skills we have already discussed, and those we will yet explore, this is a fundamental behavior for the successful manager. Similarly, motivating is inherently linked to controlling and delegating (the former is covered further on in this book; the latter was covered in the previous section). As a consequence of motivation's importance and connection to other core competences, it is also tied to your personal efficiency and effectiveness; if you have a highly motivated and active team in your control, you will simply accomplish more with that organization. Therefore, if you want to get such results from your team, you must motivate them. Indeed, the more expert you are in motivating your team toward excellent performance, the more easily and effectively you will achieve your goals.

Remember, this book will not teach you the skill of motivating; it will merely highlight its importance, provide a concise summary of it, and then enable you to assess your current skill level and design your plan accordingly.

What Is Motivation?

Motivation is about stimulating individuals so that they willingly and effectively accomplish the results you need. As an effective manager, you'll have a large number of tasks and objectives that must be accomplished, predominantly through the direct work and effort of individuals and teams in your organization. So, inevitably, if you have many (or even just a few) individuals needing to come together to get you these desired results, you had better have a method for getting them on board as willing and effective contributors.

Motivating is an essential managerial behavior, but it does not come naturally to all managers. It requires your thoughtful construction and implementation of an overall environment that stimulates enthusiastic participation. So an important part of your work becomes defining appropriate methods and then driving that motivation which propels the organization forward successfully. In short, if you want to prove yourself as an effective manager, you are going to need to showcase your skills as an adept motivator.

Overview of Training and Tools

Much of the literature available suggests and describes approximately seven areas in which you should be skilled in effectively motivating others. These are always assembled, grouped, and presented in different ways, but normally repeat the same content, with only small variations in attention to details. Motivating is a powerful tool, and even individuals who are highly proficient in the associated skills can always benefit from revisiting the supporting behaviors in order to hone their practices.

Effective training and tools should include the behaviors and practices described below. Let's outline them so that you can more easily determine whether you need to further develop this skill. (Again, the aim is not to teach you this skill, but rather to provide a sufficient summary to enable you to assess yourself and plan your self-development accordingly.)

The Best Motivator

Firstly, it is important to understand what defines **the best motivator**. Although everyone is different, most current surveys and beliefs rate "personal praise" (especially from a direct boss) as most valued by employees, above cash and all other incentives. So we begin by considering our key people individually and understanding what type of motivator works best for each of them, and for the group as a whole. Everyone in the organization needs motivators, which are always best delivered shortly after results are achieved. Remember, the manager has the *primary impact* on how happy and motivated his or her team will be.

Personalize the Motivator

The next important issue is how you **personalize the motivator.** It is better that any motivator or incentive comes from the manager, rather than from some obscure committee, program, or executive. Tie recognition to a worker's actual results and achievements in order to receive the strongest appreciation from him or her. Again, offer the motivator close in time to that worker's achievements. Build trust and a sense of security, and always be sincere in your dealings and personal communications. Learn to be comfortable just saying "thank you."

Public Recognition

A strong opportunity for motivating achievers is by providing **public recognition.** Wherever possible, congratulate in group or staff meetings, general gatherings, company newsletters, and even internal notices. Allow achievers to stand up and be acknowledged, but remain sensitive to those preferring less-public displays. Put congratulations and acknowledgments in writing wherever appropriate. Use all the types of praise that are at your disposal.

Simple Motivators Are Well Received

As a priority, always remember that **simple motivators are well received.** Much can be accomplished by sharing company information, performance, and results. Spend time listening to and speaking with employees; give of your time. Involve people in decisions that affect them, and create an environment that's open and receptive to people's ideas. It is wise to encourage and facilitate personal development and growth, not only through assignments and personal empowerment but also through training. Always provide regular, ongoing feedback and personal encouragement while employees and teams are moving toward results that will be rewarded.

Employee perks such as bagel or donut days, free coffee, workout facilities, annual group and company parties, etc., all provide their own type of motivation to the work environment.

Rewards Are Motivators

Most types of **rewards are motivators,** regardless of when they are offered. So be diverse and frequent with your recognition and rewards. Ensure you remain evenhanded with all employees, and make sure you "catch people doing things right." Both compensatory time and flexible hours are strong and simple motivators. Spot cash rewards, gift coupons, or even symbolic certificates, etc., sometimes prove to be well-appreciated motivators as well.

Formal bonuses that measure performance goals are always well received, and they can enthuse participants. Just be sure to balance these with personal praise, opportunities for growth, and employee involvement programs.

Motivating in Negative Situations

A skilled manager should even be capable of **motivating in negative situations**. When things aren't going well, provide guidance and goals with appropriate support for success. Be clear about nonperformance, but motivate even modest performers to improve. When it is just not working out, you have to let people go; a tolerated poor performer will even provide serious demotivation to some achievers.

Money Is Not King

And lastly, always remember that **money is not king**. By all means, build a comprehensive scheme of basic monetary rewards and motivators that drive enthusiasm for the work and workplace. However, separate rewards for special achievements from the paycheck. Create an atmosphere where people can extend themselves exceptionally to contribute, without fear of failure and retribution. Finally, get that essential and necessary buy-in to your rewards and recognition schemes, and then monitor the effectiveness. (Buy-in must come from your boss, your peers, and your subordinates—all with differing levels of support and commitment, as appropriate.)

The above overview is very brief, yet respectably comprehensive, and it provides an economic use of your time. Generally, presenters and authors in this area often do not provide significantly greater content; rather, they tend to dwell on broadening the descriptions of the individual elements and pointers provided above. Certainly, those more extensive discussions of motivation should help you better review your practices and assimilate your thoughts. The important issue is that you now have a meaningful overview of the skill of motivating, which will enable you to review what is involved in motivating others so that you can better assess your own current level of accomplishment (or need for development) in this area.

Do You Possess Motivational Skills?

It's usually pretty easy to tell. Just run through the bolded items above (under "Overview of Training and Tools"), and it should be clear. You have a pretty well-motivated and empowered team, or you do not. Again, you must know if you are spending your time with individuals and if there is a positive outcome for those involved. Are they motivated? Are they getting results? Is it apparent they feel free to offer suggestions and make recommendations? Most simply, are there events and circumstances where you are openly recognizing accomplishments and rewarding the participants?

If you have built (or are in the process of building) such an ideal environment, all these things will be readily visible. Better yet, you will already feel a sense of personal accomplishment in having established such a workplace. You will know if you are comfortable interacting with people in such an outgoing and supportive fashion.

Should these behaviors and practices be absent from your organization and/or indeed feel uncomfortable to you, you need some self-development in order to progress toward those more senior positions you desire—and indeed for your own personal development as both a manager and an individual. And, if this is this case, it would then be appropriate for you to seek some direct training or more information on the subject of motivating, as it would indicate a deficiency in this skill (in an honest self-assessment, if the latter is true for you, you would need to score yourself as currently poor in this skill during the assessment below).

Assessing Your Current Skill Level

Just score yourself excellent (E), average (A), or poor (P) in the total set of behaviors and practices described above (bolded items under

"Overview of Training and Tools"), and then keep a record of your single score in the skill of motivating by making a note on Table 6A in part II, page 142. We will assess later if this should be a priority self-development area for you.

Reference Materials

A great starting place for studying this subject is in basic, general-purpose management-development books or articles. Extensive online options are available if these, or the basic overview offered above, are not immediately sufficient for your needs.

Good online search terms include: *motivating employees, employee motivation, management and motivation, motivating in management,* and *motivating workplace.*

Key Points to Remember

Every manager must be a good motivator! Motivating, controlling, and delegating are essential managerial skills that inherently work in concert. Keep in mind that money is not the only—or the most important—motivator. Always acknowledge achievements in a timely manner. Praise must be sincere and publicly visible in order to be effective short- and long-term. Never underestimate the importance of saying "thank you"! The simplest motivators are often the best motivators. Making your skills as a motivator visible and well-known will serve to showcase your lead candidacy for your targeted position.

Planning

The Importance of Planning

This is an area that is often not treated in a particularly formal and organized fashion. Quite often, organizations and individuals are eventually trained in this skill by consultants brought in to "correct a situation," or perhaps by senior managers who are ultimately forced to implement their own structure for the organization. For our purposes, we will discuss a more formal process, which is in no way a methodology or scheme intended to provide a quick fix, one-off action, or a remedy that could (and often should!) be addressed in a more ad hoc fashion, or at least by "other methods."

Without a formal planning process, an individual manager, and/ or his or her organization, will be truly adrift. Their actions cannot normally be tightly tied to, or thoughtfully coupled with, the needs and strategic vision of the larger organization. Even the smallest group of individuals can benefit in performance by spending time in effective planning, which, in turn, will ripple down and positively reflect in their day-to-day activities and the goals they pursue. So it is important for every effective manager to understand the nature and value of planning, as well as what it can and should entail. Certainly, we do not always find organizations, or even companies, that are truly well planned and organized. Sometimes this is simply caused by lack of knowledge, but other situations are symptomatic of pure laziness and/or suggest an immaturity of focus. The truth is, effective planning techniques require real leadership and organizational skills, which, in turn, will establish a robust and well-integrated process.

Remember, this book will not teach you this skill; it will merely highlight the importance of planning, provide a concise summary of it, and then enable you to assess your current skill level and design your self-development/career plan accordingly.

What Is Planning?

Planning is about establishing a common organizational vision, sharing that vision, and aligning the supporting team with short- and long-term objectives that ensure the vision is realized. Realistically, unless you have well-aligned and well-planned goals in place, it is unlikely that you will achieve your targeted vision with any degree of precision. Why would you even expect a specific and ideal outcome without following some reasonably systemized approach?

Some individuals tend to be natural planners, but they are the exception rather than the rule. Most folks find the discipline a little tedious; they may even consider it "hard work." However, if you have complex needs or prevailing business conditions and/ or a substantial organizational structure, planning is the key to precisely targeting the most valuable objectives required to achieve your vision for the future. So we see that planning, too, is a critical management skill.

Overview of Training and Tools

Many of the books and much of the training materials available tend to discuss and review those concepts that are involved in planning, rather than suggesting any specific or useful structure. The points made are pretty universal and may be grouped in as few as four or five categories. These are always useful to understand and inspect in detail. However, the simple descriptions provided below provide a more organized and coordinated view of what planning can offer, as well as outlining its benefits and the actual structure(s) and discipline(s) involved in its successful implementation.

Effective training and tools should include the behaviors and practices described below. Let's outline them so that you can more easily determine whether you need to further develop this skill. (Again, the aim is not to teach you this skill, but rather to provide a sufficient summary to enable you to assess yourself and plan your self-development accordingly.)

Types of Planning

Firstly, we should consider the **types of planning**. At the highest level is the *strategic plan*, which establishes the organization's mission and vision, outlines its overarching objectives, and recognizes prevailing and changing conditions. This includes finances, customer needs, competition, timing requirements, etc. Once the vision is set, an *annual operating plan* (a second, separate document/plan) can then be created to detail the short-term actions and measured goals for the group(s) involved. The annual operating plan must support the needs, vision, and direction of the strategic plan.

Purpose of Planning

The next important issue to consider is the **purpose of planning**. We must thoughtfully condense the vision of the strategic plan right down into supporting, day-to-day objectives and actions listed in the annual plan, and even further into individuals' goals. Planning's purpose is to set direction, recognize obstacles, agree upon solutions, and achieve consensus. It ultimately reduces the organization's actions to a simple set of measurable goals to pursue. Finally, we must put "triggers" in place to reset plans in the event that circumstances change and plans need to be revisited.

Discipline of Planning

Little will be accomplished unless we regularly respect the **discipline of planning**. Planning is normally repeated regularly every year, with the team revisiting the overarching strategic plan to "set the stage" (often, this merely requires minor retouching or revamping), and then moving forward to develop the coming year's detailed annual operating plan. All major contributors to the elements of each plan must participate at their appropriate levels, as personal and organizational buy-in is essential. Ultimately, define only a manageable set of the highest-priority reasonable and measurable goals within the annual plan, and then ensure that they all offer maximum return for the investment.

Following the Plan

Next, it is essential that we are **following the plan**. A review process must be put in place to monitor plan performance. Each annual operating goal should be reviewed weekly, and/or monthly, and/or quarterly, depending upon what best fits each goal's importance and volatility. Establish and maintain appropriate forums—from one-on-ones to group quarterly meetings—that will effectively monitor performance in achieving measurable goals. When critical plan elements are not being accomplished, the organization (or individual) must adjust, as required, in order to correct such discrepancies. As always, the plan must be supported, and so resources should be adjusted appropriately, wherever necessary, in order to achieve the overarching and most-important goals.

Sharing the Planning

Finally, there is the critical step of **sharing the planning**. Most people normally like to know what's going on and how they contribute to the team. Management must communicate a simple and complete strategic vision throughout the organization. The detailed annual goals and supporting actions should be routinely and thoughtfully tied to the overarching strategic mission/vision, as this will ensure buy-in. Share and communicate quickly to get everyone on board; discuss and share with energy, enthusiasm, and commitment. Only a well-communicated strategic mission/vision and supporting plan will be enthusiastically embraced and supported.

The above overview is quite brief. It nevertheless offers true insight into how an effective planning process can be implemented. Again, this is provided in a form that ensures the effective use of your time. Authors and trainers in this area often do not offer substantially more than is overviewed above. Actually implementing a meaningful, well-organized planning process is a major project. It is not for the unskilled or the faint of heart. However, once in place, it provides the necessary infrastructure and mechanisms to efficiently direct and monitor the organization, while simultaneously targeting and accomplishing substantial objectives, all of which can be tightly aligned to that guiding, long-term vision.

Again, it is important here that you understand what is involved in the process of planning so that you will be able to assess your own skills. There can be variations of the degree to which the structure described above is implemented. These may be driven by your own position in the organization, the size of the organization, and/or the freedom you have to implement your own structure. Nevertheless, the basic principles apply, and the inherent structure described is sound for almost every situation.

Do You Possess Planning Skills?

As always, this is pretty easy to determine. Just run through the bolded items above (under "Overview of Training and Tools"), and it should be clear. You are spending time developing and implementing plans, or you're not. You have an operating structure that is aligned with a strategic vision and is actively supported throughout your organization, or you do not. Lastly, you have a set of personal and group objectives that are aligned with and toward a strategic vision, or you do not.

Generally, good planning practices are evident and readily observable in any skilled manager's behavior. If you are not demonstrating these types of skills, or are uncertain about how to approach implementation, you probably should consider some form of training or investment for your personal development. You do not have to climb very far up any management ladder before planning skills become an essential part of your repertoire.

Assessing Your Current Skill Level

Just score yourself excellent (E), average (A), or poor (P) in the total set of behaviors and practices described above (bolded items under "Overview of Training and Tools"), and then keep a record of your single score in the skill of planning by making a note on Table 6A in part II, page 142. We will assess later if this should be a priority self-development area for you.

Reference Materials

The entirety of the description provided above already quite comprehensively discusses the basic principles involved in the planning process. Within this general description the basic process and intentions are quite adequately presented. However, numerous other online resources, websites, and tools are available that can provide supplementary insight and knowledge that you may determine is required for your particular self-development purpose.

Good search terms include *planning, business planning, business plans, business plan basics, strategic plans,* and *operating plans.* Take particular care to understand the very specific knowledge you personally need regarding planning *before* you begin the search process; this is necessary in order to avoid exploring materials and topics less-relevant to your particular needs.

Key Points to Remember

Planning is a critical managerial skill that involves engaging the team in supporting and implementing the organization's mission/vision. First, managers must establish and implement a long-range, overarching strategic plan (mission/vision), and then they must design an annual operating plan that ties the long-term vision to day-to-day working practices and activities. Inevitably, all managers must display an effective planning skill set, and visibly doing so will increase your value as the lead candidate for the position you seek.

Organizing

The Importance of Organization

Again, a plethora of materials are available in this area, and the subject has many very capable and well-published authors. Interestingly enough, as teaching material, this seems to be an area less focused upon as a stand-alone topic, but rather a subject often tacked onto generic training classes. Oddly, when written about, "organizing" is often almost treated as something of a lifestyle preference for effective living, rather than an essential, adoptable behavior that professional managers must learn to leverage for everyday use at the office.

Most of us can enhance our personal efficiency by being "better organized." Yet, surprisingly, there is generally little to no training in schools or universities to prepare us to make sensible judgments and efficiently order our professional activities and work space. Similar to the generic activity of "reengineering" (covered separately later on in this book), the skill of organizing can dramatically improve the effectiveness of any given individual. So it is certainly worth quickly reviewing the discipline, skills, and considerations involved, assessing your own current capabilities, and determining how improvements in this area might enhance your overall value and competence.

Remember, this book will not teach you this skill; it will merely highlight the importance of organization, provide you a concise summary of it, and then enable you to assess your current skill level and design your plan accordingly.

What Is Organization?

Organizing is about operating efficiently and leveraging effective systems. The reality is that we all work in environments where systems pass information and data to us which we, in turn, must assimilate, classify, plan with, and act upon. Essentially, we are individual parts of larger systems, yet normally no comprehensive handbook is available to us that comprehensively defines our required behaviors and actions as managers inside the boundaries of what we receive and generate. Basically, you're on your own to figure out what to do and how it should be done. So it is essential that you have the ability to recognize what might be accomplished more efficiently, have the ability to define how to do it, and then, finally, be able to plan and implement all those systems necessary to accomplish those important results. Like many other skills discussed in this book, "organizing" is a critical competence to develop and master.

Overview of Training and Tools

The materials on this topic are always grouped and presented in different ways, but they will typically address the same issues, concepts, and behaviors you will need to develop in order to be an effectively organized management professional. Effective training and tools should include the behaviors and practices described below. Let's outline them so that you can more easily determine whether you need to further develop this skill. (Again, the aim is not to teach you this skill, but rather to provide a sufficient summary to enable you to assess yourself and plan your self-development accordingly.)

Benefits of Organizing

The first thing to consider is the **benefits of organizing**. Generally, these include more personal time, productivity, and efficiency. Further benefits include less stress, with accompanying better health and improved professional image and personal relationships.

Personal Discipline

Next is the issue of **personal discipline**. It is a fact that anyone can learn to be organized; this is a skill and behavior, not a genetic attribute. Certainly, it is easier for some than others to commit to changing practices that cause clutter or disruption. It is important in this process to set goals for improvement and to allocate time for planning prioritized improvements. At the core of this skill is the need to increase focus and energy on critical issues and real results, and to avoid time-consuming and wasteful activities.

Target Problem Areas

As we begin the process of organizing, we must **target problem areas**. This is done by searching for observable and/or reported disorder, such as paper stacks and piles, complaints, expressions of unserviced needs from others, etc. Similarly, events that disrupt and interfere with focused productive work also qualify as problem areas requiring organization. We must categorize and sort all incoming information and data so that it is addressed at appropriate and convenient processing times. Lastly, you must set aside dedicated time to implement those new systems that you plan to use in order to better organize your projects, your work space, your routine, and yourself.

Organizing the Work Space

As we begin to make improvements, it is inevitable early on in the process that we focus upon **organizing the work space**. The basic rule to employ is, "out of sight, out of mind." Stated another way, the principle is to "use it or lose it": discard items used rarely or easily and conveniently retrieved when needed. Often-used supplies should have ready access and storage spaces; drawers and cabinets (and even their electronic equivalents) need spacers and organizers. There should always be orderly filing with a simple retrieval process, where only those items that need to be accessed frequently are visible and on hand. Desks and walls should get equal respect, with each having low occupancy and no clutter. These aforementioned rules apply equally to the electronic systems and information used within the work space (including both their internal setups and their displays).

Development of New Systems

Critical to success is the **development of new systems**. The world is comprised of interrelated systems. Our own systems should be well defined and efficiently planned, while simultaneously being as efficient, maintainable, and simple as possible. It is imperative that we ensure information and data flow easily from one place to the next, and that they are appropriately discarded when future usage is minimal. When a repetitive or routine activity can be improved upon with a good return on investment (ROI) vis-à-vis your and/or your team's time, it should be automated directly or moved to the best place to implement that improvement.

Integrating the Work Space with Electronic Systems

In today's office it is imperative that we carefully **integrate the work space with electronic systems**. Work space, desk, fixed computers (desktops), and mobile computing devices (laptops, communicating devices, etc.) all must work together seamlessly in order to be individually efficient and collectively functional systems. We should process information where it serves us best, from paper on the desk, to data in electronic databases, to e-mails on mobile computing devices, and so on. Optimize the space for all your activities: a desk that matches your needs, seating that is comfortable, and equipment/supplies that are placed conveniently. As applications and new products emerge, reconsider your entire system for potential to improve efficiency; today's world offers rapid technological advances and constant opportunities for improvements.

Organizing Travel and Commuting
Outside the office we should ensure that we optimally **organize our travel and commuting**. Always pack like a minimalist: carry only extras for likely circumstances, and leave the kitchen sink behind! Choose whether you will work in transit or not, and make realistic plans for when that work might occur at times which are both convenient and achievable. Always empty the briefcase (or carry-on) of everything that isn't essential, usable, and readily accessible while in transit. Use hands-free, voice-based tools whenever safe and efficient, and only rely on "setups" (writing tools and/or computing) that have some certainty of being deployed conveniently in readily available locations while you are in transit.

New Gadgets and Applications
Finally, keep an eye open for organizational opportunities emanating from **new gadgets and applications**. At the same time, remember that all that is new is not always ideal for your personal systems and modes of operation; some products just turn out to be toys rather than truly useful tools. Assess individual benefits and functions, and then objectively integrate viable new items or clinically cast them aside. We should adopt only those new tools where they naturally fit the way we choose to operate, are convenient to our purpose, and offer us some real and measurable advantage.

The above overview is very brief, designed and provided for the economic use of your time. Diverse perspectives are offered on the subject of organization. Indeed, for some authors, this behavior is the "center of the universe," and skills such as planning, controlling, and delegating are subordinated as just "supporting activities." Clearly, all these behaviors are closely related and integrated in day-to-day use. Nevertheless, it is certain that all managers must have a well-developed ability to organize both themselves and those they manage. It is imperative that you generally understand the skills of organizing so that you will then be able to assess your current capability, especially in regard to the need for your improvement in that area. You will definitely bring more value to your career by further development of this behavior.

Do You Possess Organizational Skills?

It's usually pretty easy to tell how committed you are to effective personal organization. Just run through the bolded items above (under "Overview of Training and Tools"), and it should be clear. You are routinely reviewing the manner and efficiency with which you operate, or you're not. It's pretty easy to recall if you have been investing time in your systems, work space, tools, and environment, and also to know how receptive you are to upgrading your practices.

You can literally see if you've set up an efficient, well-organized, uncluttered office/work space and have appropriate technology engaged—or if you do not. Last of all, if you know you are not a particularly well-organized person, you probably should invest in some type of training or tools in order to ensure that you experience those very real health, reputational, and relationship benefits that will result from some personal development in this area.

Assessing Your Current Skill Level

Just score yourself excellent (E), average (A), or poor (P) in the total set of behaviors and practices described above (bolded items under "Overview of Training and Tools"), and then keep a record of your single score in the skill of organizing by making a note on Table 6A in part II, page 142. We will assess later if this should be a priority self-development area for you.

Reference Materials

You can readily find any number of books available on the subject of organizing. Books are dedicated to the subject if you want to explore it in depth. More likely, you will benefit most from leveraging those materials that provide a substantial section on the subject in a general management context. It is important to make sure the book you use is adequately business-centric and provides the depth of review that matches your particular development needs.

Key Points to Remember

Organizing entails the behavior of operating efficiently and leveraging effective systems. It applies to individuals, teams, work spaces, routines, and projects. Therefore, an effective manager must be a good organizer. Organizing is a readily visible essential managerial skill, so displaying it positively will likely increase your value in terms of your lead candidacy for your target position.

Controlling

The Importance of Control

A lot of materials are available that describe this skill. Realistically, any successful manager will be prone to exhibiting a high degree of "control." Almost inevitably, this is typical of a highly driven professional, but the lightness of the control asserted relative to the magnitude of the results achieved is perhaps the truest measure of a polished manager. This is another discipline well worth reviewing, as it is a fundamental, day-to-day behavior required of every manager and leader. Let's quickly review what is involved and proceed to a personal assessment of your own current capability in this area.

Remember, this book will not teach you this skill; it will merely highlight the importance of control, provide a concise summary of it, and then enable you to assess your current skill level and design your plan accordingly.

What Is Control?

Control is about influencing and securing an outcome without necessarily *personally* executing any or all of the tasks required to achieve that result. By definition, controlling is inherently tied to delegating, and as a result, some of the description is common to both skills. Many personality types inherently exhibit high tendencies toward control. This can be a good or bad thing (and sometimes even a liability), depending on how that control is exhibited and exerted. Certainly, all capable managers must routinely utilize the skill, and those personalities that specifically lack the "controlling" characteristic will inevitably need to develop themselves in this area.

Overview of Training and Tools

The training materials and literature available in this area describe much the same behaviors and practices, regardless of their source. As usual, these may be presented in different ways, but the general description provided below provides a solid summary of what is required for an individual to develop the right tools, practices, and behaviors in regard to control, and thereby to become a more successful manager and leader.

Effective training and tools should include the behaviors and practices described below. Let's outline them so that you can more easily determine whether you need to further develop this skill. (Again, the aim is not to teach you how to develop this skill, but rather to provide a sufficient summary of the behaviors to enable you to assess yourself and plan your self-development accordingly.)

Trusting Employees

Firstly, there is the issue of **trusting employees**. This means that you must effectively empower others to succeed. Regardless of whether you hired or inherited your direct reports—and regardless of whether you do or do not particularly like them—you should provide opportunities for them to spread their wings and pursue objectives that can develop them personally and enhance their capabilities. All leaders must be given enough rope and guidelines to make meaningful progress, but not so much that they can hang themselves or derail a program that may be critical to their own (or your) success or image.

Getting the Best Result

The next critical matter is about **getting the best result**. The solution achieved may not always be exactly the one you wanted, expected, or even anticipated. However, as long as it satisfies the mission's goal(s) and is a robust and workable solution, it is a good result. Try never to derail or heavily redirect a team or individual working toward a defined goal, unless it is essential. If you must take this type of corrective action, you must also ensure that everyone remains well motivated and effective.

Defining Cost, Time, and Extent Criteria

To move effectively toward a defined goal, you must have comprehensively **defined cost, time, and extent criteria**. It is imperative to establish clear objectives and goals up front. Define the available resources, and be available to counsel promptly in order to ensure efficient, frustration-free progress. Such established criteria must be monitored minimally but adequately, and preferably only when reviewing the project's progress.

Measuring Progress

A key to success is **measuring progress**. Reviews should be minimal, but they must occur at regular, relevant, and important intervals. These reviews should ensure adequate insight so that errors, misconceptions, and misdirections can be fixed without embarrassment or serious losses. Minor errors can, and often will, occur. Only then is it important to correct, adjust, learn, and quickly move the team forward on a positive note.

"It's Not about You"

To ensure success, it's imperative to understand that **"it's not about you."** Many individuals in your organization have valuable suggestions and sometimes even better ideas than your own. Perhaps you could sometimes achieve a better or faster result working alone, but then you would not be able to contribute as effectively elsewhere. Well-guided, empowered teams can bring to the organization excellence and diverse thought from varied backgrounds, and this allows them to achieve exceptional results.

Direct Personal Involvement

Sometimes it is essential to have **direct personal involvement**. This should only occur when your skills or embedded knowledge offer such overwhelming advantages that it is wasteful for you to stand aside and operate through pure delegation. In this event, the rules are much the same: ensure you have adequate time and resources to succeed, and define the goals and desired result(s) in the same manner. Still, you should hand off all that can be delegated, and you must also establish a minimized mechanism to monitor the progress and availability of the support that you will require. For a seasoned manager, the do-it-yourself (DIY) approach should truly be a last resort.

Celebrating the Results

Once successfully achieved, be sure to **celebrate the results**. Individually acknowledge all those involved, with words, appropriate rewards, and celebrations. Be sure to communicate the success of individuals and/or teams outside of the immediate group. Also communicate relevant information and knowledge that must be shared for any new processes, procedures, approaches, etc., that have been developed.

Control Is about Results

Lastly, it is crucial to remember that **control is about results**. Working through others extends your reach and capacity. Achieving through others means sharing the credit; do so generously and equitably. When employees succeed, so do their managers. Remember, relinquishing direct control of details is another fundamental tool of an effective manager, and it works in tandem with the core managerial competence of delegating, as described at the beginning of this section.

The above overview is quite simple, yet comprehensive. Writers and trainers in this area often provide more detail, but perhaps not much more substantial content than is offered here. Control is an intriguing area because it is seemingly assumed to be an inherent skill, rather than one that should be routinely and comprehensively taught and learned. This is somewhat anomalous, as individuals who strongly demonstrate this behavior often need guidance in toning down their methods so that they can more effectively work through others. Similarly, individuals lacking such strong instincts are not offered broad and relevant guidance for development. Suffice it to say again that the balanced and thoughtful use of control is the mark of an effective manager.

Do You Possess Control Skills?

It's usually pretty easy to tell the strength of your ability to control by simply running through the bolded items above (under "Overview of Training and Tools"). Results coming from an organization can range from regular, significant, and timely to minor, unpredictable, and infrequent. If results don't happen, it can be from lack of planning, structure, commitment, poor morale, etc. Generally, managers who exhibit control tend to plan, coordinate, and follow up in order to achieve those results. However, the skill with which they wield their control will affect the quality of their results. A heavy-handed "control freak" may achieve significant results but may also have a seriously demotivated team with uninspired commitment over the long haul. This can ultimately be as detrimental to an organization over time as an ineffective manager who exhibits little to no control, existing on the unpredictable and poorly directed commitment of hardworking individuals on his or her team.

Objectively review if you are exhibiting well-balanced control. Do you get timely results on significant objectives? Do your employees remain enthusiastic, motivated, and willing? If your review of these questions is positive, you need consider no further development of your control skills in your current position. Now consider further that *future* job you seek. Are your current practices and skills properly aligned for that role? If not, more fine-tuning, study, and practice may be required to prepare you as the ideal candidate for that desired position.

Assessing Your Current Skill Level

Just score yourself excellent (E), average (A), or poor (P) in the total set of behaviors and practices described above (bolded items under "Overview of Training and Tools"), and then keep a record of your single score in the skill of controlling by making a note on Table 6A in part II, page 142. We will assess later if this should be a priority self-development area for you.

Reference Materials

A great starting place for studying this subject is basic, general-purpose management-development books or articles. Extensive online referrals are available if these materials, and/or the basic overview offered above, are not immediately sufficient for your needs.

Useful search terms include: *management controls overview, organizational control techniques, controlling management examples,* and *controlling management.*

Key Points to Remember

Control involves the ability to influence and obtain a desired outcome without necessarily *personally* executing any or all of the tasks required to achieve that result. It is inherently linked to the skill of delegating, and the two behaviors work in tandem. The ability to exert control with finesse is the hallmark of effective, skillful managers, so showcasing your ability in this regard will lend strength to your appearance as preferred choice for the promotion you desire.

Reengineering

The Importance of Reengineering

Oddly enough, and quite disappointingly, not many materials published in this area are suitable for "everyday use." The technique of reengineering is indeed potent, and one would naturally expect it to be featured in many management-development training course materials, or even in personal-development materials. However, this is not typically the case.

This should not minimize the importance of the topic. Reengineering affords all levels of managers, and even supervisors, the opportunity to take a fresh look at what they're doing, how they do it, and how and where they can improve. Potentially, reengineering offers the opportunity to make dramatic improvements to the current situation. This is not something that is applied to tune up an established process or situation; rather, it is an opportunity to radically influence the status quo and to make major progress in improving established norms.

As time progresses, most institutions and organizations continue to build upon existing infrastructure and ways of operating. So the bigger your organization and the longer you've been around, the more likely it is that you will have systems ready for, and in need of, a radical overhaul. However, it is also the case that small, new, and even entrepreneurial organizations can benefit dramatically from this process.

Needless to say, those individuals who see the opportunity and bring the insight for such improvements are the very people we need driving organizations. So reengineering an area of work, a process, or a system is a great way to improve your situation and promote your own value at the same time. Spotting such opportunities is one type of value, but actually leading the team that gets the results is demonstrating an even higher level of competence.

Remember, this book will not teach you this skill; it will merely highlight the importance of reengineering, provide you a concise summary of it, and then enable you to assess your current skill level and design your plan accordingly.

What Is Reengineering?

Reengineering is about looking at the current situation, reducing it to a process, and then massively improving the efficiency of that process. The results sought when reengineering are always truly major, as opposed to small improvements or refinements. Typically, when reengineering a process, the goal is to improve overall effectiveness by 50 percent or more. Indeed, if it is practical and feasible, goals of 100 percent—or even tenfold—improvement may be sought. Using this approach, such results have been successfully attained and shown to be viable.

To reengineer a situation, simply reduce the activities and dependencies to basic flow diagrams. Define the current process so that the existing situation can be recognized and documented, and then brainstorm creative methods to redefine an enhanced flow. With that accomplished, improve this flow in the best way possible, now using concepts, facts, materials, and resources that are already available or that can be readily made so.

When reviewing the processes and practices surrounding your current situation, it is sometimes shocking to realize the obvious inefficiencies and opportunities for reengineering that lay right in front of you!

Overview of Training and Tools

The primary materials available describe the process of reengineering by considering six steps. Sometimes these are described in different ways, but the basic flow and content outlined below will provide you with a readily understandable approach to the process.

Effective training and tools should include the behaviors and practices described below. Let's outline them so that you can more easily determine whether you need to further develop this skill. (Again, the aim is not to teach you this skill, but rather to provide a sufficient summary to enable you to assess yourself and plan your self-development accordingly.)

Understanding the Need and Opportunity for Reengineering Improvements

Firstly, there is the issue of **understanding the need and opportunity** for such improvements. You should review your operation and then compare the current situation with the possible improvements that might be attained if radical improvements could be made in any given area. Where is the biggest payback or return on investment (ROI)? Are there cost improvements, time-to-delivery, or product performance opportunities, etc.? Alternatively, do you have processes that are troubled, unpredictable, random, poorly defined, or simply undocumented? Could any or all of these benefit from a major upgrade? Pick an area that is ripe for improvement, likely to give you great payback/ROI, and certain to drive you and your team into the process and mind-set of reengineering, as and when other opportunities emerge.

Setting the Goal

The next critical issue is in **setting the goal**. Reengineering is only warranted for radical change(s) or improvement(s), such as:

- Greater than 50 percent reduction in costs or time-to-market, *or*
- 100 percent (or more) improvement(s) in some other characteristic(s), etc.

Considering the foregoing, you must set goals up front, whenever possible. Share these with your team, and communicate the intent to all those involved. It is imperative that you cement the focus and set a clear objective for all individuals involved. The initial goal defined may be refined and made more precise as the work progresses. However, at all times the objective must be clearly visible to every participant. As always, buy-in and commitment are keys to successfully reaching the goal.

Picking the Team

As you are setting an initial goal, you are also **picking the team**. You will want folks who are motivated, and you should select the minimum set of participants that can clearly articulate the current situation and help decide where changes are possible. Teams as small as two or three, or up to a dozen, are normally viable for one leader. If the process under review requires many more (perhaps many tens of participants are involved), then segment the process; set well-defined, individual team goals; and have carefully partitioned interfaces. You must pick a respected leader (ideally, yourself) to run and motivate the team, chart the current situation, and help plan and define improvements.

Evaluating and Mapping the Current Situation

Execution begins by **evaluating and mapping the current situation**. Here, the team should enter all major steps on a commonly viewable chart or screen, and then indicate time and/or costs involved, as appropriate. Ensure the flow is accurate and shows where events begin and end, including all dependencies. Keep the team assembled for sessions of tolerable and efficient meeting durations until the current process is documented. Be sure to insert the level of detail that is only to the point where insight for change is possible, and where the team can complete its work in a reasonable time frame. Review the final result and record the current time/costs situation, so that the team has a common view that allows them to see both the existing current liability and the opportunity for improvements that are at hand.

Rebuilding the Flow

Next is the opportunity for **rebuilding the flow**. The team should review what is currently being done and look for all potential opportunities to revamp the flow. Start all events at the earliest possible time, combine operations, and focus on shortening time (or minimizing cost), as required. Consider new approaches, and challenge status quo. Move activities to run parallel to others, or place them before other events, where possible. Eliminate what has become redundant. Finally, review the new flow, confirm its correctness and viability, and promote the improvements within, and outside of, the team.

Revising Procedures and Training Affected Players

It is good practice to always close the reengineering process by **rewriting procedures and training affected players.** Document the new process, and present it to all individuals who will be affected by, or benefit from, its existence. Update all internal procedures and/or training that will need to reflect the improved flow and changed situation(s). Organize training for all participants who will need such education. And, importantly, measure the current results, show the new results, and display the success visibly—this is a huge motivator. The reengineering process used to obtain the results should itself be promoted, so as to further encourage such activity and the search for other similar improvements possible across the organization.

The overview presented above provides a very brief and simple description of the practice of reengineering. Indeed, the process and method are quite simple, and they can be effected quickly within any organization after acceptance and buy-in for implementation have been obtained. Far more extensive descriptions of the nuances and implementation details are available from published books on the subject, as well as from individuals who can provide formal in-depth training. Again, it is important that you understand the nature, power, and value that reengineering can bring. Once you do, you will be empowered to judge your own skills and determine whether you need any development in this competence.

Do You Possess Reengineering Skills?

It should be pretty easy to tell where you stand with the skill of reengineering. Just run through the bolded items above (under "Overview of Training and Tools"), and it should be clear. You are able to construct such programs and execute such processes, or you are not. Are you able to define a need or opportunity, set up the team, articulate the objectives, and drive the process through to a result? If not, you could benefit from development in this area.

Perhaps you do not need all these individual reengineering skills. It may be that just your ability to spot the opportunities, point them out, and commission teams to execute them is more than enough for your purposes. However, it may be that the skill of leading such teams is the greatest value you can bring in your current situation. In such cases, look at your position and evaluate what would be of greatest value for you to bring to the table. Certainly, having a truly complete set of reengineering skills to recognize, initiate, and execute would ideally be in the repertoire of every manager and executive, but the issue is, do you currently need to demonstrate all the component skills required to drive this entire process?

Assessing Your Current Skill Level

Just score yourself excellent (E), average (A), or poor (P) in the total set of behaviors and practices described above (bolded items under "Overview of Training and Tools"), and then keep a record of your single score in the skill of reengineering by making a note on Table 6A in part II, page 142. We will assess later if this should be a priority self-development area for you.

Reference Materials

A number of print books, e-books, and audio books exist on this subject. Several profound academic articles have also been offered on this topic. However, if you have real needs to develop useful, hands-on techniques, you should research further options. Good online search terms include *business process reengineering* and *reengineering (manufacturing)*.

In this particular case, it is again important that you select and target very specific materials for your further review *after* careful consideration of your personal need to practice, excel, or undertake meaningful activity in this area in the future. This precaution will avoid wasteful review of material not truly essential to your personalized self-development plan.

Key Points to Remember

Reengineering is a complete overhaul that entails examining the current situation, reducing it to a process, and then massively improving the efficiency of that process. However, be aware that reengineering is normally undertaken to achieve radical change(s) or improvement(s)—greater than 50 percent reduction in costs or time, or 100 percent or more improvement in some other metric. It is a major undertaking but a core management competence. A visible, meaningful display of reengineering skills may well increase your value as primary choice for the managerial promotion you seek, and even for executive positions.

Team Playing

The Importance of Team Playing

This area, too, is well supported with materials and information provided by capable authors and experienced trainers. Interestingly, when formal management training is provided in companies it is often centered on, or beginning from, a need for "team development." Whether companies are beginning the development of an individual or taking remedial action, they are invariably focused upon improving teamwork and cooperation within the organization.

All top management performers should be skilled in leveraging teamwork. So, here again, we will quickly review the disciplines, skills, and behaviors that define effective team playing. This review, in turn, will either help you recognize a need for self-development in this area or simply confirm your existing abilities.

What Is Team Playing?

Team playing is about both being a good team player yourself and being able to build and operate effective teams within a company or group. The overview below provides simple descriptions to help you evaluate not only your personal skills as a team player but also the skills you possess that will enable you to set up and run teams (most often led by others) in the organization. As always, if you wish to leverage and maximize your reach and influence, it behooves you to strongly grasp the principles of team playing, and to be able to practice and demonstrate those critical skills in the day-to-day operation of your group.

Overview of Training and Tools

Most of the skills and subject areas of team playing can be condensed into just three components. Writers and presenters of materials in this area will typically group the information they present in different ways, but the basic content and subject material should not vary much from what is concisely offered here.

Effective training and tools should include the behaviors and practices described below. Let's outline them so that you can more easily determine whether you need to further develop this skill. (Again, the aim is not to teach you this skill, but rather to provide a sufficient summary to enable you to assess yourself and plan your self-development accordingly.)

Being a Team Player

Firstly, there is the issue of whether you are **being a team player** within your organization. Curiously, most people who are promoted will show good leadership and organizational skills. However, in most every situation, even if you are "the boss," you still have a boss (i.e., company owners must "answer to" customers, and CEOs must satisfy the board of directors and stockholders). Thus, in order to be successful it is also necessary to be a good individual team player when asked (or when needing) to be one. Oddly, the very personality traits that accentuate strong leadership can in some ways conflict with the ability to be a good team player. A good team player should be able to take instructions, appreciate constructive criticism, and fulfill a supportive and subordinate role within a team led by others. It is often the case that a more egotistical individual may struggle with this behavior.

Investors' Interest in Teams

Next, it is important to understand **investors' interest in teams**. "Investors" may take many forms, ranging from external venture capitalists (VCs) to more-senior internal corporate managers. In either case, three things normally matter to prudent investors: (1) the team's track record (what have they accomplished?), (2) the team's ability to work together (do they get along well?), (3) the team's ability to adapt (how well do they adapt to changing business goals and situations?). So those empowering and/or financing enterprises or programs (i.e., "investors") are keenly interested in the composition of the team. As a participant in any management team, you need to be seen to possess strong and flexible team-playing skills, as well as the ability to define, commission, and effectively operate appropriate teams.

Expectations of Empowered Teams

As we now focus on the creation of teams, we should consider the **expectations of empowered teams**. Again, being able to establish effective teams must be a priority for every successful manager. The typical benefits resulting from the creation of such teams include the following:

- Motivated participants
- Access to ground-level ideas
- Environment of sustained progress
- Nimble action
- Ability to adapt
- Improved communications

In addition to creating the above-captioned benefits, effective teams free up the manager for higher-level tasks.

Minimal negatives are associated with such teams, including (1) the requirement for deft management and overseeing, and (2) the necessity of making ongoing adjustments to minimize overshoots in mission and/or responsibilities taken on by the team.

Clearly, any management overseeing must not damage the motivation of participants and leaders. Also, motivational rewards and recognition must be incorporated into the team's operation. Examples of such teams are "quality circles" in Japanese industry and their counterparts in the United States; these are particularly visible in the automotive industry.

Types of Teams

Next are the **types of teams** that might be established. Really only two basic types of formal teams generally are initiated by management. Firstly, there are formal *tiger teams/task forces:* groups temporarily established in order to address specific issues and/or resolve specific problem(s), within established timelines, resources, and goals. They may be cross functional or organizationally vertical in focus. Secondly, there are formal *standing groups/committees:* these continue, through time, to fulfill a mission or set of responsibilities. They, too, have specific problem(s) to attack, with specific resources and goals, but without a specific time frame; they may also be either cross functional or vertical in their focus.

Additionally, there are also informal teams; often self-assembled (but sometimes created by management) and occasionally with ad hoc participation from within the group. Such teams are good for facilitating informal communications and motivating those involved. They are capable of identifying underlying problems and highlighting concerns to management. Their nonformalized nature means results are unpredictable, as no specific goals are assigned, unless one of the formalized team types described above is subsequently created to seek specific results. Examples of such forums would be discussion groups organized around specific issues or particular professional disciplines.

Developing a Team
Once we have defined a specific need, the next step is **developing a team**. To ensure success we must be sure the right leader(s) is (are) in place, the issues are explained, the resources are made available, and the mission and goals are clearly defined. After commissioning, there should be regular, adequate yet unobtrusive overseeing, without undue direction. The team must be kept on track; you should revisit assignments and resources if circumstances change. It is imperative to remove obstructions and impediments faced by the team, and to encourage thoughtful risk taking and team action. Lastly, always showcase the team and their results when needed; recognize and reward the team appropriately and in a timely manner.

Providing the Environment for Successful Teamwork
From the outset, we must ensure we are **providing the environment for successful teamwork**. It is common for teams to identify new tools and practices needed to make best progress. You must facilitate access to and adoption of these new tools and practices in order to ensure both their progress and their ultimate success. Insert essential knowledge and know-how into the team; talks, trainings, and/or skill-development programs may be appropriate. Encourage essential structure in order to manage the team's work: record keeping, action item (AI) taking, information dissemination, etc. Ensure the availability of basic operational facilities: meeting rooms, teleconference access, videoconference tools, etc., as

the situation demands and in ways that the company can make available. Ensure all participants have adequate time outside of their routine operations to fully support team efforts. Similarly, ensure all key participants, and even occasional contributors, can be available whenever required. It should be noted here that a truly empowered team will feel comfortable requesting the facilities and needs described within this section.

The above overview provides a very brief description of team playing, presented concisely for the most economic use of your time. Interestingly, authors and trainers in this area provide little more substantive information; rather, they present detailed examples and exercises for you to practice in an effort to develop your skills. Exposure to high-quality team-building activities and training can be a real eye-opener. As in other sections within this book, those simple phrases, descriptions, and principles described above might be understood more profoundly when experienced in a formalized team-building environment. Nevertheless, all the basic principles involved in team playing are revealed in the above overview. Many of these principles do warrant careful review and close consideration. Take particular care to be both objective and critical when assessing your current skills and/ or need for development in the area of team playing.

Do You Possess Team-Playing Skills?

Perhaps in this instance the answer to this question is not quite so easy. However, as usual, just run through the bolded items above (under "Overview of Training and Tools"), and it should be relatively clear. Firstly, you are personally participating as a mature, willing supporter within the (management) team where you reside, or you are not. So are you, yourself, a good team player? Also, are you demonstrating those management skills required to define, successfully implement, and operate empowered teams? Are you comfortable you are able to make the right moves, exhibit the essential good judgment required, and execute effectively to create good teamwork and successful teams? You are doing these things competently, or you are not—but, as stated, it might be more difficult to answer these questions than those posed in counterpart sections. Finally, you must now make an overall self-assessment of your current skill level in these dual team-playing roles.

Assessing Your Current Skill Level

Just score yourself excellent (E), average (A), or poor (P) in the total set of behaviors and practices described above (bolded items under "Overview of Training and Tools"), and then keep a record of your single score in the skill of team playing by making a note on Table 6A in part II, page 142. We will assess later if this should be a priority self-development area for you.

Reference Materials

If you need somewhat greater investment in this area than the outline provided above, you can consider books or courses. Generally, good search terms include *team player business, being a team player,* and *teamwork in business.*

This is invariably a good subject for a course or class, particularly if done with colleagues; such classes often prove to be good bonding and awareness-enhancing experiences.

Key Points to Remember

Team playing is a critical skill for every manager. Not only does it mean that you need to be a good team player, it also means that you need to be able to effectively manage teams within your organization. When executive management and outside investors examine the effectiveness of teams within organizations, your visibility as both a good team player and a good team leader will enhance your candidacy for the position you have targeted.

Leading

The Importance of Leadership

Here is another subject with a wealth of available information, written by academics, researchers, psychologists, trainers, biographers, and more. In the context of our overview, leading is inherently linked to and integrated with many of the other sections already covered, such as motivating, problem solving, controlling, delegating, and team playing. It is important to understand from the beginning that our discussion here will involve how to empower you to become a great *manager* rather than optimistically—and idealistically— seeking to turn you into a great *leader*! A real difference exists between these two roles, which we shall later explain to avoid any confusion in meaning.

So let's consider the skill of leading by quickly reviewing the behaviors involved. This will enable you to assess your own current level of performance so that you can determine any possible self-development necessary to fuel your career. Remember, this book will not teach you this skill; it will merely highlight the importance of leadership, provide you a concise summary of it, and then enable you to assess your current skill level and design your plan accordingly.

What Is Leadership?

In the context of our discussion, leading is about effectively utilizing the broad skill set required to be a successful and well-regarded manager. Keep in mind that effective leadership should be strong but not tyrannical. Workplace tyranny does not breed loyalty or even respect. A good leader must motivate and inspire, not terrify or browbeat. Again, we can see how applying the combined use of several key managerial skills—leading, delegating, controlling, and motivating—all will serve to increase your effectiveness as a manager.

To a certain extent, some of these other managerial skills might appear to all be part of "good leadership." Consider the old adage "lead, or get out of the way." Inevitably, it is expected that managers are able to lead effectively. If you cannot demonstrate a sufficient number of related skills combined with a general ability to lead, your career as a manager will be greatly limited. So we can clearly see that leading is indeed another critical skill.

Overview of Training and Tools

Most materials, books, and courses on this subject are presented from highly diverse points of view. Authors, writers, and trainers develop and publish leadership-related works for any number of worthy reasons. However, for our purpose, we need only care about the simple definition of what "leading" should be relative to the skills that enable a successful management career. So we will need to establish the essence of the skill itself, thereby immediately avoiding any ongoing confusion between what it means to lead as an effective manager and what it means to be is a great leader. The concisely presented sections that follow will provide the requisite clarification and description.

Effective training and tools should include the behaviors and practices described below. Let's outline them so that you can more easily determine whether you need to further develop this skill. (Again, the aim is not to teach you this skill, but rather to provide a sufficient summary to enable you to assess yourself and plan your self-development accordingly.)

The Successful Manager versus the Great Leader

Firstly, let us consider the situation of **the successful manager versus the great leader**. You do not need to be a great leader to be a highly successful manager. A great leader embodies numerous uncommon and often inspirational personal traits, such as vision, enthusiasm, confidence, decisiveness, optimism, and above all, integrity (at least ideally). Successful managers practice good behaviors and skills, such as planning, decision making, communicating, delegating, motivating, etc. (basically, the essential skills described throughout this book!). Truly great leaders are few and far between; whereas, successful managers abound. There are many great managers in industry, yet very few great leaders in business or elsewhere.

General Elements of Leading as a Manager

Next, it is important to understand the **general elements of leading as a manager**. A successful manager should be sufficiently able to effectively practice and use the skills outlined in this book. He or she should always be acting and dealing with others in an atmosphere of openness and integrity. It is prudent and useful to study and strive to emulate great leaders. Certainly, you should seek to embrace the best traits they share, all of which are commonly accepted as extremely worthwhile. The traits of great leaders that are most useful to successful managers are visionary thinking and positive outlook. Nevertheless, do not let lofty aspirations of becoming a great leader in the future overshadow your immediate need to be a successful manager in the present.

Skills of Leading for Successful Managers

Lastly, the aspiring, well-rounded individual should seek to practice the **skills of leading for successful managers**. When developed, these skills will include the ability to:

- Communicate and listen
- Share leadership role(s) and responsibility(ies)
- Support and facilitate
- Reward and acknowledge success
- Take corrective action where necessary
- Plan, measure, and monitor
- Actively motivate
- Install and operate essential structure(s)

This overview is certainly both very brief and highly concise. In many cases, purely for the sake of brevity, simple descriptions and phrases imply and encapsulate extensive supporting details not provided (or repeated) here. The description above will at least frame the subject area of leading, allowing you to assess your current level of ability in this area. Accordingly, you should evaluate if your skill set is sufficient, and if it is not, you should identify those key elements that you would benefit from developing, either through study or training.

Do You Possess Leadership Skills?

It's usually pretty easy to tell. Just run through the bolded items above (under "Overview of Training and Tools"), and it should be clear. You are practicing the generic skills that constitute effective leading, or you're not. In this case, there is indeed a large list of skill types to assess, but they are all clearly and individually presented for your review.

Assessing Your Current Skill Level

Just score yourself excellent (E), average (A), or poor (P) in the total set of behaviors and practices described above (bolded items under "Overview of Training and Tools"), and then keep a record of your single score in the skill of leading by making a note on Table 6A in part II, page 142. We will assess later if this should be a priority self-development area for you.

Reference Materials

Numerous classes are available on this topic, many of which are offered online. All such courses are of varying duration and sophistication. The subject of *leading* and *leadership in business* is particularly easy to search online (italicized terms here should suffice).

Similarly, a range of publications are offered on the subject, which is also invariably covered in the context of most general-management books. So, if you seek only a simple primer offering just a little more than the description provided above, you will be well served to review a basic general-management text.

Key Points to Remember

Avoid confusing being an effective manager with being a great leader. To lead effectively as a successful manager, you must employ in concert the essential skills of delegating, controlling, motivating, team playing, problem solving, and so on. When these work together seamlessly, the overall image is that of successful leading/managing! It is worth your while to showcase your leading skills if you want to stand out as the best candidate for the promotion you desire.

Mentoring

The Importance of Mentoring

This subject area is generally not covered, reviewed, or written about in any exorbitant depth. After all, it is probably assumed that those individuals capable of mentoring others normally enjoy significant management stature already and are more than capable of figuring out how to go about the process with little documented help. Interestingly, as the business pace has genuinely—and quite excitingly!—accelerated significantly thus far in the twenty-first century, there is perhaps now an even stronger argument than ever before that those more skilled and seasoned practitioners need to pass on lessons earlier to their successors, as doing so is essential to advancing the growth of managers beginning their careers.

My inquiries suggest that managers in most industries have seldom entered into any mentoring arrangements; nor have they been requested to do so, for the most part. When mentoring is well established, it is most commonly in larger corporations. The reality is that mentoring others not only ensures improved growth for those being mentored (mentees), it also directly rewards those wise and energetic enough to provide the service (mentors). It would also

114

seem that small, nimble, and/or high-growth enterprises should possess a similarly (or perhaps even greater) enthusiastic need for creating such personnel advancements. So, again, let us quickly review the discipline and see where you sit in regard to providing such guidance to others.

Remember, this book will not teach you this skill; it will merely highlight the importance of mentoring, provide you a concise summary of it, and then enable you to assess your current skill level and design your plan accordingly.

What Is Mentoring?

Mentoring is about a more-senior manager providing valuable insight, recommendations, and/or guidance to one more junior. It certainly should never appear to be organizational intrusion, personal coercion, or "black ops"! This is a service provided in an open and convenient fashion to encourage the career success of a promising candidate. Mentoring should always occur outside of your direct management reporting chain, and it should not be confused with coaching, which is a responsibility that a manager has toward his or her own employees and direct reports.

Intriguingly, such willing help provided to others invariably has benefits for the giver, too. Providing such valuable and far-reaching influence across an organization will show the mentor to be a strong player who demonstrates advanced management skills. Importantly, it is not required for you to be at the top of any particular management ladder in order to participate in a mentorship program and to provide effective mentoring to others.

Some organizations engage in "reverse mentoring." This is a situation where a more-junior person teaches skill(s) to one more senior (i.e., a manager), who, for example, might be taught a basic software tool by an individual contributor. In our discussion, however, we will review the more typical scenario of more-senior mentor and junior mentee.

Overview of Training and Tools

Those materials that do exist and are commercially available can be quickly summarized in six categories. A number of these information sources are more focused on very particular details of mentoring, but for our purposes, it is wiser to cover the overall topic in a short and readily consumable overview.

Effective training and tools should include the behaviors and practices described below. Let's outline them so that you can more easily determine whether you need to further develop this skill. (Again, the aim is not to teach you this skill, but rather to provide a sufficient summary to enable you to assess yourself and plan your self-development accordingly.)

"Why Be a Mentor?"

Firstly, you might ask yourself, "**why be a mentor?**" Perhaps many reasons could be considered, but mentoring certainly highlights your own value and enhances your image. It enables you to share skills, experience, and knowledge, rather than metaphorically filing them away in a dusty, unused cabinet. Mentoring empowers you to build long-term future alliances and organizational reach. Finally, it facilitates company insights at lower levels and in other operational areas.

Basics of Mentoring

Let us now consider the **basics of mentoring**. Mentoring programs can be officially company sponsored or individually driven. There is the matter of whether you mentor internally (inside your own company) or externally (into another company). Generally, it is more helpful to mentor within your own company, but external mentors are useful when the recipient needs skilled outbound guidance into an industry or business setting where there is little to no existing competitive situation. For our purposes, we will assume that the prospective mentee is always within your own company but outside of your direct management chain. This further assumes that you will be able to provide good insight, with valuable history and examples for the mentee's area of operation, after having secured any necessary permission(s). Certainly, you must be at least "one level up" from the mentee, but two or more levels will typically bring the advantages of broader insight, greater management support, and wider perspective.

Finding the Right Mentee

To begin with, there is the matter of **finding the right mentee**. Good prospective mentees show generic promise, have obvious upward mobility potential, would benefit from advice, and can accelerate their progress as a result of mentoring. They should have genuine interest in and understanding of the value of the process. Finally, they must possess good judgment and communication skills, be good listeners, and clearly be capable of accepting and leveraging candid assessment and input.

Terms and Conditions of Mentoring

Whether we recognize it or not, there really are **terms and conditions of mentoring**. This is a relationship with an unwritten contract. There are normally regularly available and predictable appointments, with random access assured to the mentee for his or her general convenience, and also to grow and build trust. Meetings should be both informal and friendly, perhaps over the occasional lunch or during coffee breaks; dinners or other social settings can sometimes be appropriate as well. Mentoring should provide feedback with immediate observations and suggestions, but occasionally brief reflective delays to check facts or supplement any input might be necessary. Privacy of discussion is implicit and guaranteed, beyond any necessary formal acknowledgment of the mentoring arrangement itself. You should begin by mentoring one person, and only move to more if you are certain that you will be able to continue to bring real value to each individual and have adequate time available.

What Is Provided during Mentoring?

Next, we should consider **what is provided during mentoring.** Certainly, there will be insight as to the workings of the informal organization versus the formal structure. As a top priority, show the mentee how to get things done, and provide examples and alternative solutions that should pay off and succeed. Pointing out the pros and cons of these alternatives is essential, as is providing insights that facilitate the mentee's acceptance of recommendations. Offering career-path suggestions is a cornerstone of mentoring; it is essential to point out the risks and gains of the alternatives. Finally, mentors are generally responsible for highlighting valuable information and resources, and also for recommending personal contacts and associations that can provide both personal growth and/or valuable experience.

End Mentoring When It's Done

Lastly, and quite importantly, you must recognize any unproductive mentoring situations, and above all, **end mentoring when it's done.** In many ways, mentoring can be like marriage: some last forever; others simply run their course. It is important to get closure if there is a need for actual cessation. Explain if circumstances move you apart, either physically or intellectually; or, if the need and value have just been outgrown. Whatever the cause, leave the mentoring relationship on a celebratory and positive note; acknowledge the gains and victories!

Again, this overview has provided a very brief and economic description. All the essential details involved in successful mentoring have been touched upon, if only lightly. Materials, books, and even organizations are centered on the theme of mentoring (e.g., Toastmasters). Mentoring is an important and valuable social aspect of managing. More than that, mentoring, when done correctly, can provide the fuel for rapid organizational development and maturation. It is important that you understand what is generally involved in mentoring so that you can assess its value for your own development and/or contribution to the organization.

Do You Possess Mentoring Skills?

Clearly, it's very easy to know if you are practicing mentoring. Just run through the bolded items above (under "Overview of Training and Tools"), and see if you exhibit the behaviors described. You are invested in this process and already practicing this discipline, or you are not. It should be equally easy to assess whether the practice should be a part of your repertoire. Certainly, if you have skills to offer and if more-junior managers in your organization could benefit from your mentoring, perhaps you should dive in and contribute in this manner.

If, however, you are doubtful of the value you might bring, it will certainly help you to review what is involved in the process, as described above. If it seems that you can readily meet these simple requirements, you should consider becoming a mentor. As mentioned previously, a mentor, too, always becomes a beneficiary in the process of mentoring. Plus, being seen to bring such an asset to the organization (without any pretension and with true value) can certainly only enhance your image as a capable manager.

Assessing Your Current Skill Level

Just score yourself excellent (E), average (A), or poor (P) in the total set of behaviors and practices described above (bolded items under "Overview of Training and Tools"), and then keep a record of your single score in the skill of mentoring by making a note on Table 6A in part II, page 142. We will assess later if this should be a priority self-development area for you.

Reference Materials

You can find extensive online support, including resources, websites, and guidance. Useful search terms include *mentoring, business mentors,* and *mentors in business.*

It would prove particularly useful to join a group should you feel you have a need for guidance, or if you prefer a framework in which to undertake your mentoring activities.

Key Points to Remember

Mentoring is a highly visible managerial behavior. Today's fast-paced business world makes it more essential than ever before, as more seasoned managers really must take a vested interest in the rapid advancement of their junior colleagues. Vastly different from coaching (which managers must do with their direct reports), mentoring offers the opportunity for you to extend your reach to another part of your organization, displaying your value to and investment in the company. Clearly, exhibiting this skill can enhance your ability to appear as the primary contender for the new position you seek.

Time Management

The Importance of Time Management

A lot of materials are available in this area, as well as a number of capable and well-published authors. Most of the courses and books focus upon attaining great personal efficiency, further emphasizing that this skill is a major component of the success of any manager or highly driven professional. We all can certainly improve our personal efficiency, and thereby achieve more through better and more focused use of our time. So it is worth quickly reviewing the discipline, skills, and behaviors proposed, which will allow you to assess your own current capabilities in this area and then determine whether you need further development in order to best position yourself as the prime candidate for that management role you seek.

Remember, this book will not teach you this skill; it will merely highlight the importance of time management, provide you a concise summary of it, and then enable you to assess your current skill level and design your plan accordingly.

What Is Time Management?

Time management is about disciplined focus, pure and simple. Individuals who are keenly aware of the time available and/or the results they need to achieve tend to be very sensitive to the limits of time. Most high achievers do, in fact, manically manage their time, energy, and personal focus; as a result, they lead very disciplined work lives. For some personality types, time management is not a desirable behavior, and in some fields it is perhaps not quite as essential. However, in general, if you wish to accomplish significant results and demonstrate yourself as a strong player in any field, you will certainly need a serious and committed level of such focus and discipline. So time management is normally a critical skill requirement.

Overview of Training and Tools

Most books and training materials will teach you how to improve in six areas. These may be grouped or presented in different ways, but they will invariably describe the same general behaviors that you would benefit from practicing if you want or need to be incredibly efficient and productive. If you already are incredibly efficient and productive, you will recognize the behaviors described as ones that you currently exhibit.

Effective training and tools should include the behaviors and practices described below. Let's outline them so that you can more easily determine whether you need to further develop this skill. (Again, the aim is not to teach you this skill, but rather to provide a sufficient summary to enable you to assess yourself and plan your self-development accordingly.)

Plan Time and Actions
Firstly, there is the issue of your ability to **plan time and actions**. This means that at the end of every day you should be reviewing

how you did that day and making your plan for the next day. In all of this planning activity, a list (or lists) of action items will necessarily abound; otherwise, how can you keep track of what you have accomplished and what you should make your next priority? So it just makes good sense to plan your progress, execute your action items, and actively check them off when completed. The idea is to begin each day with a quick review of your important goals, and then you simply get the day's work under way. You should understand how to readily set goals and put together a simple action-item list.

Focus
The next critical issue is how well you **focus**. You should be doing one thing at a time, and whenever possible, you should avoid deteriorating into inefficient multitasking. Avoiding distractions is critical, and you should have a clear, organized work space. A space that is organized for efficiency and economic activity is crucial, as it will allow you to accomplish your tasks and goals without the disruptions that will inevitably dilute or destroy your focus. (For more details, see the section on "Organizing" earlier in this book.) Basically, if a task or project is not your main priority, delegate it to a direct report or pay an outside contractor to do it, if warranted. It is critical that you remain focused during your work time.

Management of Your Energy
Along with the maintenance of your focus comes the **management of your energy**. You need to practice healthy eating and exercise regimens to maximize your daily energy. Also, recognize whether you are a "morning," "afternoon," or "evening" person in terms of your highest productivity. You should only schedule tough tasks and challenging elements at those times of day when you are at your peak, performance-wise. Less-essential tasks and activities can be sandwiched into parts of the day when you have time available but when optimal focus and thought are not critical. Taking breaks

throughout the day is mandatory in order to avoid lack of clarity; on any given day, you should only schedule the specific number and types of tasks that are achievable and essential for you to accomplish *within the course of that day.*

Avoiding Time-Wasting Elements

Critical to efficiency is **avoiding time-wasting elements**. Obvious items in this category are watching TV, surfing the Internet, and playing electronic games. You can engage in these activities any day you wish, but you should limit them to appropriate times outside of your workday. Clearly, any work activities that require Internet searches or viewing specific televised events are separate issues. However, when used as "break time" entertainment or time-killing practices, these elements are essential to avoid, as they can easily derail the best-planned and most-focused work time.

Leverage Technology

An obvious winning strategy is to **leverage technology** whenever possible. Technology offers a vast array of time-saving options, and it behooves you to avail yourself of as many of them as possible, whenever it is feasible to do so. This can mean using office tools, such as speech-to-text software, or simply (safely, privately, and considerately) using hands-free headsets to efficiently place mobile phone calls during transit times. While such times might not be part of the workday proper, they can free up your work time considerably. Tools and technology are continually evolving, and both simple and complex items for the office are constantly becoming available. Review them very selectively, and then use only those that truly help you to make your behaviors and work space more efficient and effective.

Mental Health

Another priority in any efficient time-management program is good **mental health.** The rule is simple: don't worry; just plan and act. You should avoid negative events, people, and conversations, as well as nonessential meetings and discussions, whenever possible. Similarly, at the end of every day when reviewing your accomplishments, you should just check them off the action-item list. Acknowledge and be glad about what you have achieved, and avoid feeling discouraged about any goals you missed achieving that day. Instead, set up your plan for the next day. The following morning, review the action-item list, and then begin. And lastly, be sure to schedule ample family and playtime!

The above overview is certainly very brief, as it is designed and provided for the economic use of your time. Writers and trainers in this area prepare and offer exhaustive descriptions detailing all the elements that are described here only cursorily, and in simple sentences and phrases. The available materials can help you comprehensively explore all the individual elements described above—and more. Such materials can also assist you with developing practices to follow in your larger workplace, your individual work space, and your interactions with others. The important issue is that you understand what is generally involved in time-management skills and behaviors, so that you will be able to assess if you currently exhibit this behavior, or if it is a critical area for you to further develop.

Do You Possess Time-Management Skills?

It's usually pretty easy to tell. Just run through the bolded items above (under "Overview of Training and Tools"), and it should be clear. You are planning your time at the beginning and end of each day and working with action-item lists, or you're not. It should be clear for you to determine whether you focus on one thing at a time, or allow yourself to be distracted and/or to deteriorate into far less-efficient multitasking behaviors.

Similarly, you know if you practice healthy management of your energy, if you exercise regularly and eat healthfully, and if you avoid time-wasting behaviors—or if you do not. You can literally see if you've set up an efficient, well-organized office/work space and if you have appropriate technology engaged—or if you have not. Last of all, if you don't have a strong and organized plan to engage in positive activity with sufficient time for family and friends, you're likely just not on the right track with time management and could benefit from development in this area.

Assessing Your Current Skill Level

Just score yourself excellent (E), average (A), or poor (P) in the total set of behaviors and practices described above (bolded items under "Overview of Training and Tools"), and then keep a record of your single score in the skill of time management by making a note on Table 6A in part II, page 142. We will assess later if this should be a priority self-development area for you.

Reference Materials

Here, you can readily find any number of books available on the subject. You can employ books dedicated to the subject, or you may simply leverage those providing a substantial section on the subject in a general-management context, if that is all you need. It is just important to make sure the book you use is adequately business-centric and provides the depth of review that matches your particular development needs.

Useful search terms include *time management* and *time management skills.*

Key Points to Remember

Effective time management is critical to success in business—and in life! Optimal efficiency and productivity lead to higher achievement and improved results. As much as it's necessary to plan in order to reach important goals, it's equally necessary to ensure sufficient time and energy to do so. Therefore, it is crucial that you present yourself as someone who effectively manages time and energy, as doing so will lend you primacy as the best choice for promotion into your desired position.

Public Speaking/Presenting

The Importance of Public Speaking/Presenting

There is certainly a wide array of materials in this area, including some capable and well-published authors, and of course, accomplished trainers. Most published materials tend to deal quite lightly and quickly with the skills required to be a good (or great!) presenter. Perhaps you don't need to be a really accomplished presenter, but in many cases, your ability to stand up in front of a captive audience and persuade them of your value, self-assurance, and competence is a great opportunity. If you have specific job prospects and management roles in mind, "showing off" on a stage is a great way to elevate your cause. At the same time, if you will need to speak to groups and audiences in that new role and are not sufficiently confident and capable in your delivery, it may be that you have a liability that must be mitigated in order for you to realize your career objective. Either way, improving this skill would benefit your future career.

Remember, this book will not teach you this skill; it will merely highlight the importance of public speaking/presenting, provide you a concise summary of it, and then enable you to assess your current skill level and design your plan accordingly.

What Is Public Speaking/Presenting?

Public speaking is all about confidence. You're not going to stand up in front of a group and speak convincingly and impressively unless you are well versed in your subject, confident in yourself, and well practiced in speaking/presenting to groups. Most high achievers and senior managers tend to have "reasonably good" to "accomplished" public-speaking skills. Much of this may have been driven by necessity, and many of them may have received on-the-job practice throughout their careers. Nevertheless, being capable in this area right out of the box, or early in your career, can only increase the value you bring to the table.

Sometimes, when a manager is very accomplished in public speaking, he or she will be called upon to deliver important messages, even when his or her discipline and/or seniority might not seem to warrant selection for that specific presentation. However, when a senior manager is responsible for a large organization (or an entire company), and a message related to that organization or company must be delivered, *that* manager will always be the one who delivers the presentation. And, in general, a strong presenter is normally perceived as equally capable in running a strong and successful organization.

Overview of Training and Tools

The books, training materials, classes, and groups available in this area will teach you how to improve in six areas. These may be grouped or presented in different ways, but they will provide you with similar descriptions of those skills, behaviors, and practices that you will need in order to achieve the level of mastery essential for you to pursue your career goals.

Effective training and tools should include the behaviors and practices described below. Let's outline them so that you can more easily determine whether you need to further develop this skill. (Again, the aim is not to teach you this skill, but rather to provide a sufficient summary to enable you to assess yourself and plan your self-development accordingly.)

Types of Messages

Firstly, there is the issue of your ability to understand the **types of messages** that you may need to deliver. Fundamentally, three basic types usually are considered: *selling, status,* and *call to action.* How you develop and actually structure a presentation will depend on the type of message, as different structures have proven more effective for each of these different message types. Also affecting your message-delivery choice will be the size of the group to which you present. Large audiences and venues permit almost a "reading" style, where you might literally deliver from a prepared script, as a lecturer might. Conversely, a smaller group setting allows you to better interact with your audience; you may even develop real rapport, as and when this is appropriate. The greater the skill of the presenter, the better he or she will be in engaging increasingly larger audiences, when required.

Planning the Message

The next critical step is **planning the message**. The way that you structure your presentation critically affects the audience's understanding, which, in turn, affects how effectively you will persuade and influence them. It is generally true that any presentation will open with a simple statement of the main argument (or point), provide evidence and proof of this argument, and then restate the original opening argument in the conclusion. Care should be taken to ensure that the overall presentation format is matched to whether you are *selling, providing status,* or *initiating a call to action,* as mentioned above. One of the greatest crimes of (and traumas to) presenters is not matching the time allotment to their delivery, so care must also be taken in apportioning time appropriately for each phase of your delivery, as this will ensure that you finish on time.

Formatting the Message

Along with planning the message based on message type comes **formatting the message.** You need to be sure to master the media you are using for your presentation(s), as the medium used for each presentation will impact the way in which you frame and deliver the message. Be sure you learn and gain sufficient confidence in any of the following presentation formats you will require: TV, Internet, radio, video conferencing, teleconferencing, and live audiences of all sizes. If you must present in a format you have seldom used before, practice ahead of time until you feel comfortable with the new medium, venue, etc. When technology is involved in your presentation format, it behooves you to be well practiced, have a qualified troubleshooter on hand, and communicate expectations to that person in advance of the speaking event.

Self-Preparation

Along with your presentation comes the necessary step of **self-preparation**. It is crucial to develop confidence so that your delivery will be polished. So you must be completely aware of every nuance of your delivery. You must learn how to relax, breathe, and speak slowly. Knowing your subject well and checking (and rechecking!) your facts will always naturally elevate your confidence. Comfort in using the message format (medium, venue, etc.) required will also boost your confidence. Nevertheless, mastering the flow of your delivery and the rhythm of your speech can only be best accomplished by diligent practice. Indeed, you must accept that "practice makes perfect"; here, repetition is key to mastery. Presenters should generally stay close to their practiced delivery and content. Following your presentation is essential, but you should be well prepared for unexpected, surprising, and even unreasonable questions, especially when a Q&A session is required.

Tools and Tricks

It is good to be familiar with the tried-and-true **tools and tricks** of successful presenters. You should always try a dry run of your delivery; whenever necessary, with a "practice audience" and with the use of a simple digital recording device (preferably video). A must for any successful delivery is the presenter's sufficient preparation and readiness for the presentation, as these breed confidence and effectiveness. So always arrive before the event, visit the physical site of the presentation ahead of time, be there early to present, and gain a sufficient comfort level in the presentation-format medium well in advance of the actual event (live or recorded). Greet the attendees as they arrive (or at the beginning of a recorded event or webinar), and grow your confidence as the moment for delivery approaches.

Dealing with Nerves

And, finally, be prepared for **dealing with nerves**. Speaking in front of an audience is perhaps the greatest and best-known of all personal fears. There are many ways to get past this problem, but they all inevitably involve getting experience in actually presenting in person and in developing presentation materials (where and when they are required). Joining public-speaking groups (such as Toastmasters) is a great way to improve your current skill level. Alternatively, you can go to classes where others seeking the same skills are willing and able to offer a safe, comfortable, and open environment that supports, suggests, and provides constructive feedback. Above all else, to excel in presenting to an audience, you must practice. The foregoing applies to recorded media engagements as well, although nerves often seem more prevalent when facing a live audience.

The above overview is brief and concise, yet generally comprehensive. A critical fact that cannot be ignored is that most management (and certainly senior management) positions will require you to present in public (or via video conference, teleconference, webinar, etc.); sometimes to very large groups. This is likely not a skill you want to be learning or developing under fire. While you may have had some reasonable past experience in friendly environments, perhaps even, say in college or during staff meetings as you rose through management ranks, this invariably does not prepare you for standing in front of (literally or virtually) new or unknown audiences who may or may not be sympathetic to your message and cause. If you work in sales or marketing, you may have already started your career with a useful skill set in play, and you may have been well practiced from the outset. In general, however, it is more likely that you will have to take the time and make the effort to refine your skills in order to better match the needs of that management position to which you aspire.

Do You Possess Public-Speaking/ Presenting Skills?

As with many of the other skills we've already reviewed, it's usually pretty easy to tell. Just run through the bolded items above (under "Overview of Training and Tools"), and it should be clear whether you are already demonstrating those behaviors and exhibiting significant awareness and competence.

An alternative, fail-safe check is to simply record a mock presentation with a video camera and then review the results. Generally, this experience is fairly sobering but always enlightening. If you currently make presentations within your work environment and have a trustworthy colleague whose honest opinion you can seek, perhaps it would be best to simply and safely ask him or her how you are doing. Bear in mind that it is better to get a relative, rather than subjective, insight. This will enable you to directly compare your skills with those of other presenters (the "competition," so to speak). Comparison with speakers already well known to you will give you a starting point from which to more objectively understand and then hone your own skills.

If you really feel that you do not need to enhance this skill right now—or for your next immediate career move—simply put away its pursuit. However, do be warned that almost every career that passes through even just a level or two of the management hierarchy will ultimately need a demonstration of some level of public-speaking/presenting skills, at least competently if not masterfully.

Assessing Your Current Skill Level

Just score yourself excellent (E), average (A), or poor (P) in the total set of behaviors and practices described above (bolded items under "Overview of Training and Tools"), and then keep a record of your single score in the skill of public speaking/presenting by making a note on Table 6A in part II, page 142. We will assess later if this should be a priority self-development area for you.

Reference Materials

Here, you should read a book or take a class (many are offered that can be readily found online), as best suits your needs. Searches for online materials are straightforward, and good search terms include *public speaking, making presentations,* and *toastmasters.*

You should consider joining a group if you need to really excel in this area of your self-development plan, or if you need to continually evolve your skill set. This is certainly an area where the opportunity to practice and take the stage will best advance your skills.

Key Points to Remember

Public speaking and presenting are skills that eventually and inevitably are necessary in every management career. Public speaking is among the most-common fears, but in this case, practice truly does make perfect. Regardless of whether you have had an opportunity to utilize these skills at work (for example, if you work in sales or marketing), you would be wise to develop or hone these skills if pursuing career advancement, as this highly visible discipline can make—or break—your chance of promotion.

Part I Summary

We have now reviewed all the fifteen essential managerial skills:

1. Specific job-related skills and training

2. Problem solving

3. Decision analysis

4. Interpersonal relationships/management styles

5. Delegating

6. Motivating

7. Planning

8. Organizing

9. Controlling

10. Reengineering

11. Team playing

12. Leading

13. Mentoring

14. Time management

15. Public speaking/presenting

After careful review of each and all of these skills—complete with your notation of your score for item 1 on Table Y (page 26), and your notations of your scores for items 2 through 15, inclusive (excellent [E], average [A], or poor [P]) on Table 6A (in part II, page 142)—you can readily view the areas in which you excel, are average (or sufficiently good), and/or are poor and require immediate improvement.

Now it is time to move on to part II, where you will complete a full self-assessment of both your current status and future needs; this is the process that will help you customize a realistic, personalized self-development plan. Armed with your customized career plan, you will be able to present yourself not merely as the ideal candidate for the position you desire but, better yet, as the inevitable choice!

Let's move on to part II without further delay.

Part II

Creating Your Development Plan

Effective Self-Assessment

What now remains is for you to completely document and understand your current skills, assess the qualifications and skills you need for your target job, and prioritize the actions you should take to ensure your methodical development (including when to best accomplish each step). This activity is stated easily enough, yet to avoid any confusion, we will provide some further guidance. So, as you proceed, part II will walk you through the entire process as a hands-on experience, providing examples that will illuminate the steps required. We will then finish with a comprehensive summary of part II and a conclusion of the entire book.

Using Your Self-Assessment Optimally

Let's consider what you have accomplished so far (through the end of part I):

(1) You have completed your profession-specific requirements (Table Y, page __).
(2) You have also identified and reviewed the essential skills required by every successful, effective manager. These are skills 2 through 15, inclusive, as described in part I.

(3) In addition, you have notated a "score" (excellent [E], average [A], or poor [P]) of your current capability/performance in each of these skills (Table 6A, below).

If you have not yet completed your self-assessment of all these skills, please do so now, using Table 6A (below).

Table 6A: Current Self-Assessment

SKILL	E	A	P	DATE*
Problem solving				
Decision analysis				
Interpersonal relationships/ Management styles				
Delegating				
Motivating				
Planning				
Organizing				
Controlling				
Reengineering				
Team playing				
Leading				
Mentoring				

Time management
Public speaking/Presenting

Key: *E = excellent; A = average; P = poor*

[* *As Table 6A is a "snapshot" of who you are in terms of your current capabilities, you may wish to include the date when you record your self-assessment score. That way, whenever you refer to it, you can readily gauge how much progress you have made since your last review.*]

[**NOTE:** *The first essential managerial skill, specific job-related skills and training, was treated separately and is not included here. Refer to Table Y, page 26*]

Keep in mind that Table 6A serves as a "snapshot" of who you are in terms of your current capabilities. You can refer to this at any time, revising it as your experience and skills develop.

Reviewing Your Current Skill Set

Now consider the skills necessary for the job you are targeting. This will include profession-specific skills (refer to Table Y, page 26) *and* generic management skills (2 through 15, inclusive; shown again in Table 6B, below). Which profession-specific skills are clearly important for you to possess in order to enhance your chances for getting your targeted job? Similarly, which generic management skills are clearly important for you to possess in order to enhance your chances for getting this same job?

In other words, now that you know who you are currently (as reflected in Tables Y and 6A, pages 26 and 142, respectively), you are ready to determine what you need to do in order to fully target the job you want. (Based on what we've covered so far, you should be able to figure out which skills are needed for your target position. If you have trouble, seek advice from your manager, HR, or any trusted colleague.)

Using your current scores in Table 6A (above), now complete Table 6B (below) in order to record which generic management skills you will need to develop so that you appear as lead candidate for your target job.

Table 6B: Self-Assessment of Skills Needed for Target Job

SKILL	SUFFICIENT FOR TARGET JOB	NEEDS DEVELOPMENT
Problem solving		
Decision analysis		
Interpersonal relationships/ Management styles		
Delegating		
Motivating		
Planning		
Organizing		
Controlling		
Reengineering		
Team playing		

Leading
Mentoring
Time management
Public speaking/Presenting

Now that you have assessed which skills you need to develop in order to secure the job you seek (Table 6B, above), remember that it is quite possible to need development in an area and yet "not care" immediately, nor pursue any corrective action, if that specific skill is not immediately pertinent to your career path. However, if you gave yourself a score of poor (P) in Table 6A and recognize that it is a critical skill for the job you seek in Table 6B, it is obviously a priority for you to develop this skill. Simply compare your scores for each skill in Table 6A with the need for improvement (or not) in Table 6B, and then design a prioritization for the development of your skills: that is, establish a list of the things you need to work on, in priority order (most-critical skill first and least-critical skill last).

Finally, referring back to Table Y (page 26), see if your current profession-specific skills are sufficient for your target job. If not, you will need to consider some development in that area as well.

Assessment Follow-Up

Using what you discovered in Table Y (page 26) and Table 6B (page 144), you should now have a short list of desired improvements necessary to pursue your target position, which we need to scrutinize further for priority. Each of these skills is summarized (in principle) in part I of this book. Now you not only know the things to work on but also the specific aspects that are of value to you. Revisiting Table 6A enables you to update your current status. So, whenever you choose to repeat this process and target a different specific position, simply redo Table Y, update Table 6A, and then redo Table 6B.

Now you are truly empowered. You know what you need to work on in the elements of specific importance to your purpose. Finally, you have access to books, papers, and all manner of training classes and materials that are available and accessible to you through libraries, bookstores, or the Internet.

Remember, the aim of this book is not to teach you how to develop any of the fifteen essential managerial skills described, but rather to enable you to assess your current capabilities and performance so that you can design a personalized, efficient, self-development plan accordingly.

Key Points to Remember

Complete your full self-assessment honestly and objectively in order to gain a realistic picture of who you currently are. This means that you will have completed the list of your profession-specific skills (Table Y, page 26) and your generic management skills (Table 6A, page 142). Remember, this is your "snapshot" that you can turn to at any point in time, revising it as your skills develop. Using your scores in Table 6A, you are ready to complete Table 6B (page 144), which will show which skills you need to develop for the job you seek. The combination of the two lists enables you to target the specific job you desire. These are your profession-specific skills (Table Y) and your job-specific management skills (Table 6B).

Dynamic Self-Development

Creating Your Customized Plan

It is important that you do *not* bury yourself in needless, in-depth reviews of any specific subject. Rather, find those areas that best suit your development needs and that can advance your skills in the immediate manner you seek—as well as in the long run. It is imperative that you move quickly to identify the materials and sources you want, so that you can swiftly embark upon an ordered and organized self-development plan. Allocate dedicated and prioritized calendar time during which you will complete your studies and self-development on a regular basis. Once you have a simple plan outlined, with an accompanying timeline for completion dates, you are more likely to follow through. So now consider Table 7 (below), where a complete example self-development plan is shown. (Note that this example would be based on your discoveries following completion of Table 6B [page 144]. It also draws from Table X [page 25] for an example of profession-specific skills that need development.) Such an example plan could take one to two years to complete; it targets the job you desire, and also positions you for further moves up the management ladder.

147

Table 7: Example Self-Development Plan

SKILL (prioritized)	Development SOURCE	Start	Complete
Public Speaking	Class (Toastmasters)	February	Aug/Sept
Time Management	Book (choose one)	April	End of April
Controlling	Audio Book (choose one)	July	End of July
Mentoring	Pool of Candidates	August	September
Assess Candidates		Aug/Sept	September
Begin Mentoring		September	N/A
WHAT'S NEEDED (prioritized)	Development SOURCE	Start	Complete
MBA	University	August	May
PowerPoint	Online class	January	February

The above example offers some interesting pointers. Note that there are many sources for information. Also, some skills need to be completed before others, not all skills have precise schedules, etc.

Your current individual skills in any area(s) may be advanced or rudimentary. This does not matter. It is just important to recognize where you are now, what you need to develop, and why. Remember that the goal is to first establish a realistic plan and then to work that plan effectively. Once the initial plan is executed, you can return to assess the defined priorities necessary for the next step in your development, or even review your entire skill set again (using the process outlined in this book).

The key is to always move forward! Just be sure to consider the best plan for you to design in order to get on track and address additional issues essential to your personal development and career goals, even if these are further in the future. Following these steps will establish you as an empowered and skilled manager.

Key Points to Remember

Having honestly completed your self-assessment, you now know who you are and where you are, skill-wise. From this point, you proceed to the next step: creating your customized self-development plan. Set up your development goals in order of priority, and schedule these goals on your calendar so that you ensure completing them on time. This will also give you the time and motivation to pursue additional self-development goals, as and when necessary and appropriate. You are now using all the tools at your disposal to function—and be seen—as a skilled and empowered manager, and ideally, as the principal candidate for any new position you seek.

Part II Summary

As emphasized throughout all sections, this book does not aim to immediately develop your management skills. Rather, its sole aim and intention is to show you how to accurately and objectively assess your current skills/capabilities, determine which areas you need to further develop, and then craft a customized plan to achieve that self-development, thereby positioning you to attain any promotion or position you desire.

Part II has shown you how to accurately and honestly complete your full self-assessment. Again, this involves your profession-specific job skills (Table Y, page 26), your current generic management skills (Table 6A, page 142), and the generic management skills you need to develop for any specific job you target (Table 6B, page 144). The complete full self-assessment shows you who and where you are currently in terms of your skills and capabilities. Knowing and accepting this will enable you to design a realistic self-development plan, and that plan, in turn, will help you optimize and achieve your career goals.

Armed with your customized plan, you have all you need to develop yourself as the ideal candidate for your target new position.

Conclusion

Congratulations! If you've reached this point, you've learned or developed skills, facts, and techniques designed to empower you to be a successful manager and to optimize your career. The lists that you have to consider—Table Y, with your profession-specific skills; Table 6A, with your scores in each of the generic management skills (2 through 15, inclusive); and Table 6B, with the generic management skills you need to develop for your target job—provide you with all that you need to assess your current capabilities and plan your future development.

Let's just briefly review the entire process of self-assessment and streamlined career planning we have completed in this book:

- Listed the most significant skills and behaviors possessed by well-developed managers.
- Explained the specifics involved in mastering these skills (but, remember, this book's purpose was not to teach you how to develop the skills you lack).
- Helped you determine your own strengths and weaknesses regarding these individual skills.

- Helped you itemize those skills you should personally target in order to support your immediate growth and career needs.
- Helped you design a self-development plan to target specific positions and manage progress along your chosen career path.
- Provided you with the ongoing ability to reassess and revisit your growth needs as they evolve in the future.

What you have accomplished thus far is a huge achievement! The skill set and methodology for continual self-development that you have reviewed in this book can serve you for the rest of your professional career. Specifically, this process will better prepare you to target and secure desirable management positions. In addition, it can benefit your personal development outside of work and/or in the creation of your own business/entrepreneurial venture.

Having made this investment in yourself, you are no longer doomed to proceed aimlessly through learning experiences that are perhaps interesting but that lack targeted outcomes that meet your goals. More importantly, you are now better equipped to methodically pursue desirable professional positions in a world that is becoming increasingly competitive with each passing year. A more competitive global market requires that you adapt how you present yourself, and consequently, that you become better prepared to purposefully attract those career opportunities you desire and seek.

All that remains now is for you to begin "working your plan." My best wishes for much success in your future career and in all your personal endeavors!

References/Resources

Books

Colvin, Geoff. *Talent Is Overrated: What Really Separates World-Class Performers from Everybody Else,* paperback edition. New York: Penguin, 2010.

Gebelein, Susan H., and Kristie J. Nelson-Neuhaus, et al. *Successful Manager's Handbook,* 8th ed. Minneapolis, MN: PDI Ninth House, 2010.

Hammer, Michael, and James Champy. *Reengineering the Corporation: A Manifesto for Business Revolution.* New York: HarperBusiness Essentials, 2003.

Nelson, Bob, and Peter Economy. *Managing for Dummies,* 3rd ed. Hoboken, NJ: Wiley Publishing, 2010.

Websites

www.toastmasters.org

www.managementhelp.org

About the Author

Ian R. Mackintosh has more than thirty years of management experience, which serve as the basis for the principles and recommendations that this book describes. Ian's mission in writing this book is to help managers of all levels effectively optimize their careers.

Well known in the EDA and semiconductor industries and an ASIC pioneer, Ian's background is in semiconductor design, software development, and business management. The founder, chairman, and president of OCP-IP, he has served on the boards of various groups dedicated to SoC development and IP exchange through open standards. He has also chaired working group activity developing standards for, and investigation in, IP protection. Since 1980, he has held various senior management positions in Silicon Valley, with National Semiconductor, VLSI Technology (now NXP), PMC-Sierra, Mentor Graphics, and several start-up companies.

Ian has excellent experience and a proven track record in running engineering-based businesses. A well-known industry veteran with notable achievements in established organizations, turnarounds, and start-ups, Ian is an organized individual with exceptional leadership skills and a broad spectrum of management experience. His proven record of management success motivated him to write this book as a way to assist and inspire other management professionals.

He holds a master of science in microelectronics from Southampton University, England.